Ancient Persian Empire -(Iran)

Diplomacy and Laws with
RUSSIA AND USA

Dr Amrit Rattan K Baidwan Macfarland

BSc, LLB, (Hons) DipLP, LLM, NP.

Doctor of Science, Master of Laws.

Gotham Books

30 N Gould St.
Ste. 20820, Sheridan, WY 82801
https://gothambooksinc.com/

Phone: 1 (307) 464-7800

© 2025 *Dr Amrit Rattan K Baidwan Macfarland*. All rights reserved.

No part of this book may be reproduced, stored in a retrieval system, or transmitted by any means without the written permission of the author.

Published by Gotham Books (April 12, 2025)

ISBN: 979-8-3485-1765-6 (H)
ISBN: 979-8-3485-1763-2 (P)
ISBN: 979-8-3485-1764-9 (E)

Because of the dynamic nature of the Internet, any web addresses or links contained in this book may have changed since publication and may no longer be valid.

The views expressed in this work are solely those of the author and do not necessarily reflect the views of the publisher, and the publisher hereby disclaims any responsibility for them.

WITH K MACH 10

Geologist, explorer, Mountaineer, Skier, Aviator, Senior Airline Captain, 757, 767, 777, 787, 320, writer and editor par excellent

In 1812, Alexander the Tsar of Russia, defeated Napoleon Bonaparte, Dauphin of France, but by then Napoleon had successfully destroyed, the unholy Roman empire, a conglomeration of nations.

TABLE OF CONTENTS

PROLOGUE

Jupiter Optimus Maximus Departure and Return? 1

USA and Iran Diplomacy 24

Diplomacy Iran, Syria, Russia 25

Iran and Usa Diplomacy as Relations. 30

Russia and Iran Diplomacy as Relations 30

Diplomacy Iran USA and JCPOA 32

Diplomacy and Terms of JCPOA 32

Diplomacy and Obama Administration 33

Diplomacy Sanctions and Trump Administration 35

Diplomatic Conceptual Paradigms and Channels 37

Diplomacy Sanctions and Other Nations. 38

Diplomacy Iran and Coercive Diplomacy 40

Diplomacy and Tests Treaty Interpretations and Legal Instruments 41

Diplomacy – Military and Cultural Civilisation Development in Iran 42

Legal Diplomatic Obligations – US Iran – Containment, Syria, Lebanon, Russia, USA, Appeasement, Acceptance of Jurisdictional Status 45

Iran's Military as Diplomacy Region Security and Defence Peace Conventions. 46

Diplomacy and Stabilisation Procedures Substantive and by Laws. 47

Diplomatic Relations Persian Islands and Expansive Empire of the East. 48

Diplomacy The Laws and Negotiations 50

Diplomacy Persian Cultural Civilizational Development in Iran. 51

II DIPLOMACY IRAN ARABIAN PENINSULA AND PARTNERSHIPS SYRIA 52

Iran Arabian State of Diplomacy 53

Syria's Conflict with Iran and Russia's Involvement. 54

Iran Arabian Procedural Substantive Diplomacy 55

Iran Arabian Limitation of Diplomacy 55

The Persia Empire as Diplomacy Russia and Syria. 56

Diplomacy and Economic Histories 57

Diplomacy and Egalitarianism 57

Diplomacy Evolving Roles of Hezbollah, Iran, Russian, Turkey 59

Diplomatic Policies Strategy and Tactics 60

Diplomatic Initiatives and Governance 60

III DIPLOMATIC PARALLELS TO EASTERN EUROPE AND WEST. 63

Diplomatic Paradigms Iran and Russia 67

Iran Russia Syria Middle East, Arabia Diplomacy- 68

Diplomacy Iran and the Formation of Brics 70

Diplomacy Iran Russia and Nato Expansionism 71

Iran Diplomacy – Escalation Zones Syria Zones and Rivers. 74

Diplomacy – Astana and Geneva Talks Ceasefire Diplomacy – Initiatives Iran. 77

Diplomacy and Recovery Programmes, Lessons from European Recovery Programme. 81

Diplomacy and The Doctrines of Balance of Power. 85

Diplomacy and The Aleppo Highway, Securing Territories. 89

Diplomacy Iran and War Refugees 93

Diplomacy Stability and Fragility Index. 96

Iran Diplomacy and Policy of Safe Zones. 104
Diplomacy And Humanitarian Crisis Iran and Russia............................. 106
Diplomacy Crisis Management Iran and Lebanon 109
Diplomacy And African Revolts Spill Into Arabia................................... 113
Diplomacy and Dealing with Common Arabian Issues Iran, Lebanon and Syria... 116
Diplomacy Iran, Iraq, Kurds, Syria Oil and Gas...................................... 120

IV IRAN DIPLOMACY AND THE IMPACT ON THE ARABIAN PENINSULA AND MNE'S IRAN AND AFRICA DIPLOMACY
.... 122
Dialogue of Christ as Roman Zeus with Solus Christos.......................... 141
Victories, War and Peace... 144
Iran and Russia 201

References.. 203
About The Book 209
About The Author.. 211

Napoleon Bonaparte – Dauphin of France,
with constitutional codes war and peace.

Napoleon Bonaparte, Madame Tussauds, London, Life Size.

Napoléon Bonaparte in Paris Chateau de Fontainebleau, and Palace Tuileries

PROLOGUE

JUPITER OPTIMUS MAXIMUS
DEPARTURE AND RETURN?

What a pair in the sun
Blazing in different hues,
Over the Cairngorms,
Mountains so fair

Lands crimson, red orange too,
Stag, Deer, in plenty!
Scorn at danger everywhere,
The towering heights,
The proud heads in humble
Resignation,
The gold glistened.
The steeds famished.
The winner's day
The bridle in rugged hands,
Gallop's strength,
Go, go, do not look back,
Lightning speed,
Titan tired with
Burning gaze,
Where are you now,
Salutes his finality

Immortal now
With majestic pride
Leaps clear.
Snorting nostrils
Echo, streams, gurgle
Delightful life returns,
The tapestry weaves and weaves,
No digressions so vile
So base,
Captain of the Fleets,
Cyclops its sharpened
Stake,
Poseidon god of the sea,
The island floating in
The sea,
The war of Troy,
The hide of bulls,
To Hermes, speedy diligences,
Circe not so fair,
Syclla, a monster
Charbiydes, too,
Plausible but not content,
The sea on the move,
Venus, opposes.
Apollo, Zeus too
Athena to the rescue
Auroclochos her man
Friday,

Syclano to one side

Nausicca to goddess Atremis,

Crete not far away

Angelic then diabolic era,

Eumaisos,

Telemachos,

The Queen of Ithaca,

Your beauty your fame,

This gargantuan estate,

Wordless stretched her string.

The roll of thunder

Antinoos, Eurymachoos,

Milantros,

Tis yours

Go rest now,

Hang up your laurel wreath,

But what you won

O force divine.

Jupiter Optimus Maximus as Benevolent Sagittarius

Edinburgh to Norway to Bombay
To Yorkshire,
Glory does not defeat,
Virtue with merits,
No price to pay,
No two in separation,
No violet ornaments
From afar no marriage sealed
As broken
No envy, no denial,
Two continents but a flight away,
The road to vineyards in the summers,
Loveliness temperance,
No empty hallways
No rough summer winds,
No darling buds of May,
No golden complexions dimming.
No fading of souls
No picnic baskets
Going missing
Christmas as frozen December
The blue eyes flying.
Home for Christmas
Saturn and Jupiter
Merge
Once more
Lily is white,

Vermilion is rose.
Drawn to each other like magnets,
We are not counting down.
To Christmas the fun of Burford
Roses,
Primroses, innocence so sweet,
Angels in the air,
Orpheus and marbles,
This powerful rhyme
Sword and fires burn.
Like the twins of Kashmir,
Resplendent figure
Eyes that laugh and burn,
Passion overrated,
Fervour of the mighty sun,
The deserts weep, but we dance,
In unchartered waters, the Everest so
Grand, Peace, passion the same
Life is not brief, like dewdrops on a grape,
A rainbow, a comet,
The setting sun, whispers in the night,
Distant drums,
Beating sudden call to go and come
Waterfall's cascading
Life is a light, and a loud clap.
Of thunder, a flight of fantasy,
Of Me and You.
Flights of speed,

Boundlessness in every sphere,
Windows with lattices,
Unlock and give way.
Wings mighty and glistening
Invisible worlds to soar too above,
Swans swimming on the river Dee,
Golden rays of sunshine,
The other swan dazzling and white lands,
A sharpened breath,
Noble climbing steep,
Mountains, eagles soaring.
To new heights,
Gusts of wind,
The fair highland Scottish song, the
Proud delphiniums stare,
The pearl glistens
On a yellow rose bud's ear.

Jupiter Optimus Maximus on Jupiter!

In little things,

In all things,

Borne on Jupiter's wings,

Triumphant, wholesome,

Colossus, as stature,

A roaring sound,

A daze of the moment,

Luminous clouds,

The detached and the non chalant,

Staking its claim,

The music of sound as

Perseus coming,

Music Music joyous

Music of the soul

Its highest Joys,

Carpe diem the gene

Code is fully unravelled,

The orient express,

This dazzling neon light

Making majestic strides,

The golden forth road bridge,

As starlight

The books of honours raised,

Ravaging time, like a lion's bite,

Living phoenix

The birdies sing,

The Seagull's capture

Leon and stig in disguise.
Past career and present
Entwining
Legal scientist
This master of mine,
The brain lends its
Character we all address,
This courtroom drama,
All winners truly know,
The skilful world of forgeries,
The smoothies tongue
Masquerading as truth,
Rhetoric argument,
Perjury,
Rhetoric goes,
Argument stays
The Kenyan leopard
As stealth in action,
Murders all her preys,
First with a gentle kiss,
The bees in collective fray,
Their platted hive,

A latticed page they call home
Kookaburra sits the kingfisher.
As Halcyon,
A tiny bird is he,
This magnificent artist,

The light hood and its horizons,
Confusing all,
Stay we say,
But then the potted paws are hot with fury
River dance as warrior flames,
Encore, encore encore,
Mufasa, Mufasa, the forests clouded,
Amy Johnson the pioneer of flight
Jacqueline K Mach 10 Brinkhurst the same
Her blissful flight,
Her legend returns,
Brotherton castle fair play
Fair play we all say.
The rocks impregnable
Marshal house, earthquake
Then a tidal wave,
The two contemporary kings
Ceasar Augustus and Marcus Aurelius,
As blade runners
Climbing to 30,000 feet
The Damocles shield
The Stig is Michael Schumacher
A Champion never beaten,
We all say, Hurrah, Hurrah, Hurrah.

Jupiter Optimus Maximus on the American Constitution
The law lords,
Favour the law lords,
The judges, in law lords' chambers,
The stars on expression,
Speech, assembly,
To be free, air quality,
And not in these spheres.
Equality, equality,
Optimus streams under
This heightened equality who dares,
Who dares,
Quashing errors,
Strict scrutiny,
The prerogative of mercy,
Judgement and mercy,
Heaven and hell,
Climate change,
Extreme weather,
Striking us all.
The Nobel Prize of Peace,
Legal peace,
On the statue of Liberty,
Oslo so tongue tied.
Hail hail the heavens smile,
Rex my bird and pet of hyper intelligence
With hidden pen in beak on war and peace,
Her velvet shining hair,

And eyes,
Their Optimus hears,
Two galaxies once collided
But they will never again
Not in this lifetime or in theirs,
Who dares, to think otherwise,
250 million light years
Away
Colliding at thousand miles per hour,
The Universe knows,
Self-doting, never defeated,
Defeating,
The stone rippling
Into the silent cosmos,
The prince and princesses,
The pauper takes all
It is time for equality,
As new on the Thames is a flame.
The flame lightly burning, glowing,
And says let it snow,
Defy time, the wintry fires are burning.
I am invincible but let me show you how.
Returning at Mach speeds
Out one door in another,
From this moment
Life has begun from this moment.
You are the one right beside you.
Is where I belong from this moment.

Onwards and forever,
The supersonic handshake
Of Maximus
Is a multiplication table?
As snow is for another day
The phantom of the Opera
Is a show we all saw.

Jupiter Optimus Maximus and Me

Jupiter Optimus Maximus
Betwixt the mountains of paradise
On earth, Jupiter Optimus maximus
And Me,
This colossal call
As the flow of Justice,
As proofs of after shocks
A spiritual rock of ages,
Work, trust, implicit trust,
Self-control, prospers,
Circles with his voice,
As gentle and commands,
This star as gigantic,
And yet a flower,
Jupiter Optimus Maximus
The happy hour, happier
Hours, await us, all eight,
We salute them all then ten.
Then who knows,
Consistent bearing weight,
Teaching us all, lightly like a flower,
This light of life,
As time draws on,
Perchance, we meet like cloudlets on skies,
Green or white, roam the woods and parks,
Jupiter Optimus Maximus and Me
Earth is earth, under Jupiter's commands,

Her hand in his,
Like Nature's open book,
The splendour falls, the green oaks,
And pines, they spread,
Till the last chance,
The last dance,
The last song, when time will come.
In 100 years, it can wait,
Jupiter this streaming
Cloud, a rising flame,
And fire,
Its divine element,
Moves earth's creation on
Jupiter Optimus Maximus
Treads on this planet,
Not as its noble type
Yes, when Time disturbs,
Jupiter Optimus Maximus
He arrives, as real Time.

Jupiter Optimus Maximus as Aurora Borealis

Aurora Borealis as Jupiter Optimus Maximus

Into great flight

The arguments of intellect

The night it gathered.

No laurels on stands

In a stranger's land

The silent snows,

The general time,

No mask or mime

Like landslides of the deep

The moon behind Aurora Borealis, upon

A hill, its murmurs in my breast

The silence as deafening upon

My neck,

The family hills, their shining sides,

A great left

A landmark as motion

Not a dance, which lightens the wood.

And the summer seeds.

Jupiter Optimus Maximus Joy

Joy, high notes, and low,
Hagerman
Bellini
Per Pieta
Jupiter Optimus Maximus too
Is a song writer and a song?
This great intelligence,
Fair and from a far
Its immortal state
That blessed state
The cycled times
The human demands,
The footsteps of life
Our will demands.
Our muses decked.
The train as express
The single soul returns
To the show
As Vienna her walls fold,
The mission of Joy
Richly brought as
Its legacies of high joy
High notes and low around the globe
From shore to shore,
His shining soloists
Hand.

Jupiter Optimus Maximus – The Imperfect Singer on the Stage

Jupiter Optimus Maximus is the imperfect singer on stage.

His beating heart

Racing pulse

But yet he the impresario

Takes centre stage.

The rhapsodies from his repertoire

Is strength in abundance?

As Love's grand wit

Nature's mind does not print.

Sweet form not norm as mind,

Eddying rivers roam,

This beauteous world

The twilight as

Blue green and marigold,

The sentences he speaks.

Soothe and save,

The songs not of a mellower change

Love matured fearless.

A richer store,

The earth embraces her faith.

As Jupiter Optimus Maximus

The imperfect singer on her stage!

Jupiter Optimus Maximus Reclaims Himself from the Deep

Jupiter Optimus Maximus reclaims.
Himself from the deep
Loss so common to the human race
And common still is this as commonplace.
The nature as phantom
Takes her stand.
Her music in her tone
Was a hollow echo.
Of her own,
Yet this helmless stand
The pleasures gone.
Return to earth.
Like a star crossed
Voyager as Jupiter
Optimus Maximus
The murmurs not of dying.
But a rising star
The sweet breath
Woven through endless skies.
From sun to Jupiter Optimus Maximus
Strong son of God, his Immortal love
This for so made.
Knowledge, it grows.
And flows
We see the light is Unbroken.
This clear harp
On slipping stones

Forecast years ahead.
The dreamy head
It glows and Blooms.
The other friends
Remains this
Gallant song
None other of earth's
Best friend as
Jupiter Optimus Maximus
The only one!

Jupiter Optimus Maximus his Thoughts So Silent Vibrant Ad White

Jupiter Optimus Maximus
A brain as cerebrum
Purkinje fibre
White matter and Gray
Neurons millions upon millions
His celestial thoughts
A thousand things he
Brings home.
A sudden hand in mine
A comrade of my choice
Is He,
The sunbeam like
Hamish and Chancer
Then motions gently.
Come and go.
But soon a stream
And stir in the air.
The wild unrest has gone,
The bastion is home as heaven.
Upon an unhappy
Bark the power to think and do.
No flashes of false
And true
With the Plan B
Of me Jupiter Optimus Maximus

Jupiter Optimus Maximus - This is my Home, My Sweet Home.

The day of delights
Pure and perfect as they can be.
The source and fruit
Of days as Jupiter
Optimus Maximus
No wandering isles of day or night
Good days we met.
Far days we said goodbye.
Earth no paradise without him,
The glory is an orb, as this the perfect star
It moves, heavens, and twirls them at his fingertips.
The birds of the air
In summer hilly woods
The green shadows
Of monkey puzzle
Trees,
These Indian seas of paper scorn,
The moon its seraphic flame
Announces his return!

Jupiter Optimus Maximus Super Travel above the Blue Beauty Below

Laugh, laugh winter is here.
Solus Invictus likes it.
As Jupiter Optimus Maximus
Paris, Barcelona, London,
Lisbon, Madrid, Tokyo,
Azores, Madeira,
Canary Islands, Verde the world
Lights up

These supersonic motions
Mach speed, missed by all,
Awaiting like Cinderella her Prince's
Kiss
Sundown the moors,
The out script in the final race me,
Large of life, experience
Soul's inner deeps
The meet, feet depict.
Return offices and suits.
That old friend
The boast of men
No spectral doubts
This upward mind
Of the much loved
Jupiter Optimus Maximus is mine.

Jupiter Optimus Maximus the Aerobatic Shows

Phoebus sound heart,
Aerobatics,
These my lady rose,
Mortals in flight as immortals,
The curtain of fame,
The earth in darkness
But with Jupiter Optimus Maximus
The fullest test
Words and wings
Richest toned that flies
The credits of human views
This immortal
From starry heavens of space
This secular abyss on earth
Its matin songs
That wake the oak.
Now clothed only with bowers of ten and fifty Mays
The sparkled green now
First no dance, song for hooded
Man as blind.

USA AND IRAN DIPLOMACY

USA wars in Iraq, Afghanistan, Libya spilled into Syria which is the centre for both the end of the wars on terrorism as declared by Russia on the 17/12/2017 and also the end of the Civil war against the Assad government but also among factions. Russia and Iran in a sense both ended the wars on terrorism-initiated post 9/11 in Syria. Thus, a stage was set where the wars on terrors streamed through Syria and lodged there threatening the collapse of Damascus. Iran played a pivotal role to prevent this.

Between the years, 2011 - 2019, the fighting from the Syrian civil war began to create anomalies, in the region including Lebanon and Iraq ISIL and Al Nusra began to fight with DPNS against Lebanon's army, Israel too conducted military campaigns, against Syria and her allies, Lebanon, Hezbollah, and the Iranian forces based on the ground and the air.

Thus, like the forty-year cold wars, held in proxy nations in the Far East, mainly the oriental world, post-World War II Syria became the battleground for a renewed cold war, between Russia and her allies, and USA and her allies. Other nations began to be gradually drawn in, such as Turkey, Qatar, Saudi Arabia, Egypt, Jordan and Lebanon. Turkey became extremely agitated, and became deeply entrenched in her petition, against the Syrian government, actively participating in airstrikes against ISIL, as part of NATO and alongside the USA led coalition.

The United Nations intervened, positively to quell the cruel unrest, but equally to prevent the conflict escalating, between the USA and allies and Russia and allies. International organisations too became active, as the civil war and Iraq/Libya/Palestine/Afghanistan, mutated into extreme and unusual forms, with the USA allies and Russia and allies' positions, hardening and getting more entrenched.

Massacres, violence, were common, as the conflict involved groups and particularly the entire world. Refugees, in their thousands, and millions began to stream out of Syria.

DIPLOMACY IRAN, SYRIA, RUSSIA

Several emerging peace initiatives, had to be launched, as the conflicts, raged on and both Astana (Russia led) and Geneva (US led) talks began on Syria with the United, Nations, being the arbiter between the two strongly held views, diagrammatically opposed in an extreme sense – with the USA supporting SDF and regime change and Russia supporting the paradigm and principle of sovereignty, of Syria as paramount and the Nation's right to protect its integrity at all times – the right to protect doctrine stemming from the sovereign rights of the State and based on statehood principles and jurisprudence and Russia reasserted that President Assad was head of Syria's legitimate government.

2017 saw an escalation in peace talks held both by the Russians in Astana and the Americans in Geneva. It is well known through politico historical records that the Ba'ath government only came to power post Syria's independence in 1963. President Hafez Al-Assad, an Alawite, became the first president of Syria with a republican constitution. President Bashar Al-Assad became the President on the death of his father in 2000. The twin towers fell in 2001 and the wars in the Middle East commenced shortly after beginning with Iraq.

Post the 2011 civil war, supported by USA and allies, a multiparty election, was held and the people's council of Syria instituted their President. Assad's father was the one who, on 31st January 1973, instituted a running constitution, for Syria. It opened the way, unlike prior frugal constitutions, to remove the mandatory operation that the President of Syria had to be a Muslim This increased the opposition by Muslims, in the region and strikes began in Hama, Homs, Aleppo and Latakia.

The four corridors of Euphrates opened up and around Damascus, a coup was organised by Muslims in various factions and groups, including the Muslim Brotherhood, and associated groups. Earlier too, historically the same government, was under siege as early as 1976 to 1982, and armed revolts by Islamic fundamentalist groups were growing pace, in this period of Syria's history. Upon his father's death, Assad and his wife,

Asma, a Sunni Muslim born and educated in London rose to serve Syria and wrung in several democratic reforms.

Critics and commentators gave him no credit in aspiring to do so. Thus, the history of opposition, by former Islamic groups of 1976-1982, grew again but with much more violent vigour, to remove him from office, but also supported by domestic Arab nations. Syria by now, was composed of mainly ethnic groups, Arab, Alawite, Kurd, and Levantine – several sects of Muslims, Sunni Alawite and Shia. Christians and Jews are recent entries.

Syria's GDP increased, compared to other Arab nations, and sub-Saharan nations under the Assad successive government. However, unemployment rates, began to increase, since as early as 2009 and several cities reported poverty rates, such as Dara and Homs.

Syria faced intense drought since 2006-2011, widespread crop failures, increase in food prices, and failed infrastructure, which were not mitigated by the spill over, from the Iraq and Libyan wars, of over 2.5 million refugees and more forming every year.

The war has a curious timeline, beginning in March 2011, with a sudden insurgency of Iraq/Libya in April 2012, ceasefire by the UN in May 2013, and further escalation witnessed from 2012-2013. Islamist groups began to infiltrate too with the fallen armies, from war zones, in record numbers from January to September 2014, and spread to Northwestern Syria, Idlib, Palmyra, Al-Hasakah, and river regions.

Russia intervention began seriously in September 2015 with partial ceasefires. Aleppo was recaptured by the Syrian government by the Russia and allies, in December 2016 and a partial ceasefire was declared at interim intervals.

Several de-escalations, zones, were constructed between April and July 2017, following the Khan Shaykhun chemical attack, the Shayrat strikes, Hama offensive and other minor upsets. Russia moved in vigorously after Aleppo and broke the siege of Dier-al Zour from the region, and Russia became permanently stationed there.

The Russian armies advanced in Hama province and Ghouta and the Turks tried to intervene in Afrin in March 2018, which resulted in further Syrian campaigns from 2018, to February 2019, against Turkish military operation in Afrin, resulting in the Rif Dimashq offensive and the Israel Syria offensive in 2018/2019.

Finally, the Dama chemical attack, surfaced in southern Syria, followed by additional; USA led missile strikes, and the southern Syria offensive in August 2018. Under the new Trump administration, Idlib province de militarisation was announced, and the withdrawal of troops, with Iraq entering the fray from September 2018, against the armies of Libya organised as ISIL, and its targets, in Syria. Russian forces became a permanent presence in Syria, backed by the Assad Government. However, the attacks by the Libya organised armies ISIL, continued unabated, from January 2019 to present. The belligerents, and various factions both foreign and domestic – and the Turkish backed Syria free army, rogue groups, the Christian militias, al Qaeda, Kurdish YDG, Shia sectarian, militias, from UK and Europe, manifested in the Syrian military and civil war. CIA operatives, USA special operation troops, began training the arm of the SDF and thousands of rebel opposition groups and forces in Syria, activated the operations, beginning as early as in 2012 but lasting till the present, in spite of interventions by Russia, Iran and Syria.

The international community reacted vociferously, as did the Arab league, European union and the United Nations. But there was no conclusion, and the skirmishes went on unabated, although the majority were quelled by the Russians and Syrians and USA and its allies too acted together in tandem against the fallen armies of Libya and Iraq as organised (ISIS and ISIL).

The military and civil conflict and war in Syria resulted in the Arab league led by Saudi Arabia and the organisation of Islamic cooperation, to suspend Syria's membership. Russia, Iran and Syria, began to veto western drafted UN council resolutions as early as 2011, and prevented additional sanctions, to be imposed on the Syrian government already in the midst of chaos, estrangement and the threat of the imminent collapse of Damascus, and the surrounding regions. These and other factors, began to weigh in, on the Syrian civil war.

Iran's Diplomacy with USA has always been hostile, it has faced sanctions, and it is the same with the European Union. The JCPOA was arrived at after years of sanctions and Iran believed that the JCPOA would enable Iran to enter a new era of civilization and improve US Iran foreign relations. Iran is a member of BRICS and has positive relations with Russia. The Arabian nations hoped that with the end of the wars on Terrorism on the 17th of December 2017 a declaration made by Russia in Syria and the end of wars in Afghanistan, and the transitional state of Arabia, this would be the consequential outcome. JCPOA enables Iran a former Persian civilisation of great note to develop its key industries and its military might. The financial, economic, military and defence situation of Iran, could be better institutionalised through the strategic change and capacity in its nuclear development. The Military and economic power would enable the nation, to rise with those of all its peer nations in Arabia and equally in the world.

US Diplomacy towards Iran has been an egregious and hostile one, with continuing sanctions and equally expanding their scope, and US constantly trying to seclude the nation for the last four decades or more preventing it from gaining collaborating with international business organisations such as the UN and EU, and this policy was overturned through the provisions of the Joint comprehensive plan of action (JCPOA). This has led to Iran's greater international presence on the worldwide stage, but also obliterated enhanced tension, intensely in the regional and international relations.

Iran's potential capacity is enormous, and this is a cause of concern for hostile nations, like Israel, European nations. Israel is deemed a traditional enemy of Iran, and the pivotal change was the JCPOA. What will be the impact of the JCPOA on Iran's and its future development as a civilised nation, in the post JCPOA era. The Diplomatic paradigm can be viewed through the libraries, documentaries data, historical sanctions, foreign policies, the impact of US sanctions on the economy of Iran, its peoples, its degradation through 4 decades, at the domestic and international levels, kind of sanctions and in the oil and gas energy infrastructure, and the arrest of financial assets of Iran, the radicalising Iran to a position of resisting a draconian superstate against Iran's sovereignty and national interests. Iran will not rise overnight with the invention of the JCPOA era; it will move Iran from its current status of hostile diplomatic relations towards one of the most enhanced military powers and returning to its former civilizational glory. What happens to diplomatic relations and the status of Iran is a moot point in the thinking of JCPOA era will move Iran from its current status of hostile diplomatic relations towards one of goodwill.

IRAN AND USA DIPLOMACY AS RELATIONS.

Iran and USA diplomatic relations have always been strained and in 2018, direct talks with USA were severed and latterly conducted indirectly through Switzerland and Pakistan. Iran is the former Persian empire, and Persia kept an arm's length with USA and was no longer viewed as a better nation than Russia and UK both colonial powers, and both overarched over Iran's sovereignty under the Shah's rule, close ties then had continued with the USA with the Shah of Persia Pahlavi's Kingdom. A reversal happened after the fall of the Persian empire after the Iranian revolution of 1979.

In the 1970's oil and gas revenues of Iran grew considerably and recently Iran became part of BRICS weakening its tie with the USA, which it viewed as a dictator nation trampling on rights as a nation.

From 1981-89, the Iraq-Iran war, USA sold Iraq dual use weapons, chemicals and deadly bio pathogens, but the war suddenly ended in 1988. An Iran air flight was shot down over the Stuart of Hormuz by a US vessel, and Bush since then engendered good will towards Iran. Later under Clinton a total embargo was imposed by American companies and so the US Iran relations soured once more. The escalations continued from 2020 to 2024, between USA and Iran.

RUSSIA AND IRAN DIPLOMACY AS RELATIONS

Relations between Moscow and Iran, have been strong. Iran was invited to join the Collective Security treaty, an organisation that parallels NATO. The outbreak of the Syria war, Iran and Russia became principal allies in the conflict, and this same alliance continued in Ukraine. The Missile defence system to Iran is provided by Russia. In 2021, China, Iran and Russia held a joint exercise in the northern Indian ocean, and sea of Oman, these although began much earlier in 2019, in the Indian ocean.

Russia bought drones from Iran, and Russia, Iran share CSTO, SCO organisations with each other. They have since co funded, gas exporting countries forums with Qatar, as Russian and EEU Eurasian Economic Union want Iran to join its community and signed free trade agreements with Iran.

DIPLOMACY IRAN USA AND JCPOA

In 2015, Iran and USA, UK, France, Germany, Russia, and China along with EU announced the Joint Comprehensive plan of Action (JCPOA). The JCPOA is a complex agreement, and resolution 2231 of the United Nations, security council was passed. The agreement was not made public and Iran's plan as submitted to the IAEA.UN Security council resolution 2231, provides a balanced report, and the implications of the agreement on the evolution of Iran, as a civilisation nation and clarifies, the areas of dispute between US and Iran. The JCPOA is intended for Iran to form the nations of the world as a nuclear power. The Provisions of the JCPOA are in line with the International atomic energy agency (IAEA) and the NPT the non-proliferation treaty.

DIPLOMACY AND TERMS OF JCPOA

On JCPOA, Director IAEA Director and the head of the atomic energy organisation of Iran ratified a plan to resolve key issues, of investigation, these were not made public. The agreement and UN security council resolution 2231, provide legal strengths and diplomatic weaknesses, and equally address larger question for the development of Iran, as a civilisation also the toxic relations of Arab nations, with Israel, and ending Iran as former Persian empire. Israel's area of dispute is of the nuclear development of Iran as nuclear power in the region would threaten its existence. The implications of the politics of Arabia and Israel enter many areas of contention within the paradigm of disputes, between USA as prime principal and Israel as its chief ally and hence agent in the Arabian Peninsula.

The focus remains of the agreement and also on noted regions of disagreement between the major powers, and the balance of power in the Arabia peninsula mainly between Arabia, Iran, and the USA and Israel as opposing in the same regional axis. The JCPOA or the Joint comprehensive plan of Action is intended to enable Iran to progress to the same state as developed nuclear powers but equally it threatens USA and Israel, Hegemony in the region and is intended to stop Iran from becoming a nuclear power like India, Pakistan, and others in Asia Major. The provisions are aimed to prevent Iran from providing fissile materials for nuclear weapons, it would violate the safeguards with the IAEA and equally the NPT the non-proliferating treaty. The agreement set deal nuclear limits on plutonium production. Limits are placed on Iran and restrictions. The Limits on enrichment, are not as robust, it permits Iran to develop substantial uranium enrichment and expands it within 10 years.

The number of centrifuges Iran would be permitted is uncertain. After 15 years constraints will be lifted. The agreement deters Iran from producing fissile material and UN sanctions could be reinstated as penalties for breaking the agreement. The JCPOA blocks the plutonium pathway for 15 years or more, equally the JCPOA limits Iran stockpile of enriched Uranium. International monitoring of Iran's nuclear programme consists of comprehensive safeguards, addition protocols and verifications measures invoking CSA and IAEA, potential for military dimensions weaponisation are investigated. A Joint commission and dispute resolution system is set up with the USA UK France, Germany Russia, China, Iran and EU no bias and with India. Under the JCPOA all of the UN sanctions will be lifted or suspended once Iran implements verifies all of its nuclear commitments.

DIPLOMACY AND OBAMA ADMINISTRATION

Theories are always egalitarian and will provide an edge for Iranian financial reenergising, and thus see a dramatic increase of Iran's power, prompting greater successes in other regions and further to fulfil its myriad future objectives. The discourse has been very enabling for Iran, to enter all the mainframe paradigms of the world. US Diplomacy towards Iran has been an egregious and hostile one, with continuing sanctions, and equally expanding their scope, and US constantly trying to seclude the nation for the last four decades, or more preventing it from collaborating with international business organisations, such as the UN and EU and this policy, was overturned through the provisions of the Joint comprehensive plan of action (JCPOA). This has led to Iran's greater international presence on the worldwide stage, but also obliterated enhanced tensions internationally in the regional and through international relations.

Iran's potential capacity is enormous, and this is a cause for concern for hostile nations, like Israel, European nations and USA. Israel is deemed a traditional enemy of Iran and has actively played a role in shaping US foreign policy as adverse to Iran's interests. What happens to diplomatic relations and the status of Iran is a moot point in the theory of the JCPOA era. The Historical nature and impact of sanctions is known for centuries albeit continuous sanctions have never been used as much in the modern age. Sanctions were applied only during conflicts never peace as a political tool to arrest a war.

DIPLOMACY SANCTIONS AND TRUMP ADMINISTRATION

US Sanctions are all encompassing against economies of countries, trade, banking, entities prior to wars and executing long after it as the nation is blacklisted by the USA.

Sanction era began more ferociously post 9/11 albeit USA imposed it on many Latin American nations before this time. Its justification is that it is a deterrent during military invasions and using many countries, sanctions have become a new norm. Sanctions however as well as being a deterrent against a state, also create civilian casualties, economic poverty, collapse of businesses, increase hunger, starvation, and destroy entire nations and are the sole cause of increasing the poverty index of nations. These factors have had an adverse effect on international transactions, sale of oil and gas, and have changed altered Iran's politics. BRICS nations (eastern orientated nations, along with Latin American African) have seen the greatest number of sanctions over lengthy periods of time, and hence these nations as reverse collectivism have found loopholes, draconian sanctions, used to thwart and impoverish the nations and their citizens.

Sanctions a thesis is anti-life, wealth, health, happiness, prosperity its felicia index of nations by more dominant nations that use it to curb the level of prosperity index of nations and rise of its people by arresting their development, success, disciplines, and innovation ability and creativity. Sanctions did not fail to impoverish Iran but they failed when the same were applied on Russia during the Russia Ukraine war, the strategy used by USA, EU, other nations, within, when assessed, shows the effectiveness or ineffectiveness of these, their costs, and how these resulted in a considerable slump in Iran's GDP, depreciating it to two thirds of its value, increasing unemployment, and arresting trade, exports, imports, resulting in the loss of billions of state revenue. Iran has been unable to access state of the art technologies, there are bank restrictions, and access to financial markets, and impacting on four main domestic services to the detriment of the people due to oil and gas sanctions. The justification against nuclear capabilities was levied as Iran being a threat to the existence of Israel now nested as a state within the intersection of Africa Arabian Peninsula. What is seen as a success by USA and EU is viewed as criminal actions by hostile alien nations by the conglomeration of BRICS nations.

Coercive diplomacy its impact is studied through the effectiveness of sanctions this involves analytical tools to assess stage I to assess, nuclear sanctions, and their role in American and allies' foreign policy. What does America hope to achieve what are its goals and objectives, how effective are they, what do they cost to impose, versus impact zero, impact or reverse onus as sanctions, back firing on sender nations, and how do they improve or decrease the competitive edge of sender nations. In Iran, based on these analytical tools, Iran its GDP rate depreciated between 12% or more. Europe suffered too as bilateral trade, and transaction between the two nations, were arrested, via exports, imports and oil exports, which impacted as the worst effect on sanctions as Iran lost billions at home, domestic revenues. Iran had little to no access to new technologies, related to development in general, but also more specifically, to defence development, and civilizational nuclear development as nation. The restrictions also hit Iran's access to markets, and the restrictions on sale of oil and gas hit is domestic and international geopolitical budgets. The analytical tools thus provided, a clearer picture of the sanctions imposed over the years by America and its allies. Finally, Iran and several nations including Russia entered into the JCPOA negotiations as a first move in the positive direction.

Diplomacy through JCPOA with key nations, had a positive impact on Iran's foreign affairs and international relations, from Persian Gulf to Asia Minor and Asia Major. The freezing of Iran's resources and assets, could then be moved to acquiring modern technologies, military defence, budgets grew, such as air and ground defence of the nation, and lending its support to Syria during its civil war and preventing the collapse of its neighbouring Arabian nation, Iran improved its navy in the strait of Hormuz, thus improving its offence defence structures as protective mechanisms. Trade relations improved as its economy and it began trading with African, Latin American nations, such as Venezuela, and others in Asian countries.

Diplomatic studies have shown that removal of oil sanctions, results in economic growth of Iran through its energy sectors, and thus has a direct impact for its GDP per capita, growth rate, and influences global oil production elevates oil retardation into markets, and reduces oil inflation at international global level, reducing the poverty of nations. Energy transaction studies do a comparative oil and gas impacts of JCPOA diplomacy, which show growth in oil production, trade, supply chain increase in GDP, and domestic welfare, increase in exports, improving the macroeconomy, of the countries and improving the state of nations with which it has built supply chains as oil and gas. Many diplomatic journals deal with the consequences of the JCPOA, and address the overall power, of Iran, in the region but more importantly on the global state.

DIPLOMATIC CONCEPTUAL PARADIGMS AND CHANNELS

Sanctions imposed resulted in the depletion of economic resources, opportunities, to bring about enhancement of economies in the country. The effect of coercive diplomacy on a nation whatever their national security interests, hegemonic or other are deleterious to the health, wealth, and life of a nation, they benefit no one including the sender nation/s as reverse onus, they too have to adapt, prevent hostilities, increase technologies personnel against attacks, hostilities, including cyberattacks serve no international or significant purpose meaning, substantive or procedural.

The sender nations may impose sanctions during peace times, which is their abuse, and criminalising nations is bad diplomacy and has reverse long time consequences, which too are deleterious in the long run, deprivation, coercion, as norm, beyond its limited shelf life as disciplinary or to arrest wars. Often it is used more as a command control hegemonic principle, creating deprivation, and or coercing, the receiving nation to alter its diplomatic policies and norms, towards its beneficiaries, or chosen select nations and or allies or events assist nations vassal states where America has special interests as ongoing investment products.

The challenges to draconian sanctions by USA and allies came from the United Nations security council nation members, itself under then norm of 60 rules of laws of nations, permissible acts of interference against internal and domestic affairs. The savagery of draconian sanctions as observed by the UN security council became multilayered over the four decades, and the last twenty they obliterated regions of activity in finance, banking, petrochemical, gold, coins, technology, metals, transportation industry, education primary, secondary, and became a brutalising force of attrition and savagery against a single nation down four decades, only gathering momentum, pace acceleration in the last ten years to exponential negative status.

DIPLOMACY SANCTIONS AND OTHER NATIONS.

Diplomacy is a game of cards, swords, attrition, savagery, brutality is caught under the paradigm of games, based on the calculator or equation of malafide or Felicia equation of what is coined a game theory of hybrid diabolical theorems.

The proposal of sanctions is based on hybrid warfare, military games, positing as rational behaviour, where the playing nations strategies, are based on an economic calculus of gain capital list calculations and thus unilateral gain and damage on receiving nation.

The incompatibility of this economic calculus pollutes the beneficial effects of good diplomacy based on solid legal principles as just and fair encoded by the rules and laws of the Felecia equation.

The economic calculus is best on simply overstating and emphasising national security above all other legal principles that govern good relations between nations and thereby by a feedback loop enhance national security, not delimit or reduce it as a benevolent beneficial factor. The costs can often outweigh any natural security benefit for the sending nation and can backfire and explode in its face as a poetic metaphor.

It activates vicious cycles of consecutive games, being played, as action and reverse negative, reactions rippling between nations a bad strategic action reaction cycles which depletes rapes both players sender and receiver often the receiver nation to such savage draconian games, digs its heels in, counters the deadly games of force, process and bankruptcy, economic collapse, relinquishes the demands placed on it, and sets up reverse onus resistance obliterating paradigms to stifle the dangerousness and malevolence of such actions. Sanction ae deemed a war on a nation as similar impact destruction of estate, properties, economies, health, wealth and life of entire indigenous communities.

According to statistics of sanctions, era, or all out sanctions raise serious ethical questions on the survival of millions of civilians of a given nation, the inhumane degrading nature on human sanctity, livelihood and life truncating it by many decades. The American sanctions followed by its allies has resulted in worsening conditions in the arena of medicine and of food shortages as the most inhumane of legal orders using the criminal laws umbrella replacing international laws as just and scientific legal principles.

These increase the cost of daily living, goods, as essential, daily necessities, as food milk, fruit, amenities of life, and general wellbeing.

Financial banking embargoes sanctions again air, sea, companies, medical instruments producing companies, caused irreplaceable anomalies, as malignancies to the civilians, affecting the health mind, mental disorders lives, life span and second hand, third hand products, at exorbitant prices, could not rescue them and their growing humanitarian crisis.

The History of four decades of ever increasing sanctions against Iran, made inroads into all of Iranian life, freezing their assets, oppressing judicial review, law entities, government, departments of legislative, judiciary, executive departments, bans of defence spending, banning them from loans and other economic interests, as the game of attrition went on and on unimpeded as a global force form, a super power nation state of fifty nations with 28 nations of the European as joint venture in the last two decades.

The profitability of companies were reduced as listed on the stock exchange little to no foreign investment, resulting in dissipation of international performances and economic problems, multispeed, exponentially, from prefixing, forgery, corruption, embezzlements, money laundering and worse.

DIPLOMACY IRAN AND COERCIVE DIPLOMACY

Exerting coercive diplomacy through multilateral sanctions by American and Europe, reduced the nation, to a shadow of its former self in spite of large oil and gas, reserves, and other potentialities.

These exhibit the mind set of American congress members and senate members through consistent eroding foreign policy towards Iran and individual nation states like Kansas as with joined in the freezing of assets of individuals, having economic trade connections with Iranian companies or even individuals.

Foreign policy as coercive diplomacy through by US congress members senate and individual member nation states.

Diplomacy in the USA is shaped by influences from society and intellectuals. In America, parties are active, the political apparatus is determined by economic and political influences, and these come from various departments as state, defence CIA USA and other regions.

Norms are created, invented, through think tanks, with various nation affiliations as foreign and these lobby and shape information council on foreign affairs, such as the AIPAC, for Israel and others besides. Diplomacy takes many forms, strategic, change, hostilities, coercive punitive policies, pre-emptive, measures, and military interventions, sovereign nations. Some hold hostile mentalities as rigid citing always national security, threats, as an excuse or pretext, others advocate moderation, and collaboration, still others are influenced by various lobbies, and their basic elements. Extremists favour, military invasions, citing always the axis of evil, as framing and have a no negotiation policy toward this horrendous enemy, detrimental to USA hegemony and dominance in the region.

DIPLOMACY AND TESTS TREATY INTERPRETATIONS AND LEGAL INSTRUMENTS

The distrust between the two nations make diplomatic relations murky and Iran's influence over Arabian nation states such as Lebanon, Syria Iraq and Yemen, and other Gulf Arab states, makes US even more hostile towards Iran. Iran continues to increase the scope of its diplomatic relation with Africa Latin America nations and latterly even European nations, UK and Germany as well as EU member nations. Iran continues cooperation with Asia countries cooperation with Asia countries India and Pakistan and as far as China and its nation states. Other Arabian nations like Saudi Arabia show increased interest in nuclear capability.

US policy towards Iran is one of containment and not appeasement and, to reduce its influence in the east, west and far east, regardless of which party comes to power. The Diplomatic stances of US and allies depends on Iran's geopolitical and strategic position, its ancient civilisation, its regional and international friendships, and JCPOA is thus backed by imagination.

Iran is one of the richest energy regions in the world, and the strait of Hormuz, is of strategic significance around the world, US prevents it from being a dominant world power in direct competition with its own oil reserves. Sanctions diplomacy coercion and intimidation has now become entrenched as an institutionalised tool in USA foreign policy. Obligations for P5+1 group remain to lift sanctions to monitor backing activities, and for all parties to cooperate in the provisions of the JCPOA. Compliance rules for monetary standards too will be a necessity, going into and engaging bodies of the UN, Arab league, but the ambiguities of JCPOA remain; normalising relations, with mutual understanding will become main frame, in a better environment, Iran and EU nations, as well as BRICS nations will forge a better era less detrimental to all.

DIPLOMACY – MILITARY AND CULTURAL CIVILISATION DEVELOPMENT IN IRAN

The foreign diplomacy changed under the Obama administration and Iran became a new focus with John Kerry. Political and economic pressures were placed on Iran due to the ability of Iran to develop its nuclear capacities for military and civilizational purposes. Hassan Rouhani was the head of Iran and Javid Zarif was the foreign minder, and the nuclear negotiations began six nations took part in the negotiations and Iran presented its model; this enables Iran to transit to peaceful nuclear capacity. The agreement JCPOA was reached on 14 July 2015 and ended arguments over its transition at the UN security council.

President Trump, however, began to undermine the JCPOA, he began to question its validity and began to impose sanctions and limitations on JCPOA. He undermined the spirit of the agreement and tried to reduce the multilateral agreement (UN resolution 2231 UNSC) to one only between USA and Iran and then to unilaterally annul the agreement. EU however, stood up for the deal along with the head of the team, US Secretary of State John Kerry. A controversy had been initiated. Normalisation of ties had begun with Hassan Rouhani, he chose constructive confrontation to limit nuclear activities taking the form of constructive collaboration, discourse even in confrontational mindsets, interactive discourse, to shift foreign policy of the 11th government of Iran. The interaction of European nations and USA had begun to converge with little relative divergence albeit different stories and positions were debated.

The First debate as Diplomacy was the success arriving at an agreement with the JCPOA. Mohammad Javed Zarif, began a new era of engagement, with the international community. The P5 plus One nation had summits in Lausanne European nations, Vienna and Geneva and other Arabian regions.

USA France, UK, Germany as European nations, met with Zarif along with John Kerry is head of the team as FM of USA to resolve the nuclear issue and negotiating teams.

John Kerry and Zarif conducted many bilateral negotiations and FM of P5 plus one nations met at the UN General assembly. John Kerry improved US and European relations with Iran. John Kerry insisted on clear identification of goal, neutral concerns and planning with purpose.

After USA presidential election and victory, of Trump, he began to convince the world JCPOA was unsatisfactory and that Iran was still a national security risk for USA and EU. These terms of negotiation began to violate articles, 26, 28, and 29 of the JCPOA. Things began to degrade rapidly between the two countries.

EU however maintained contact but USA dissociated EU financial sector not to cooperate with Iran, but EU countries remained adamant stating threat cooperation was of mutual interest to both.

Zarif continued congenial diplomacy with EU member states. He met with, the High representative for foreign policy of EU and FMs of France, Italy, Germany, Canada, and France as well as other EU nations heads. Federica Mogherini was the high representative of EU for foreign affairs and security policy – and European nations aligned with John Kerry to begin the implementation of the JCPOA using multilateral diplomacy. France emphasised the importance of JCPOA for the future and good of Iran. Iran and France met in Brussels.

The US government under Obama and John Kerry, conducted further summits with mutual respect. Obama as President of USA at the time, waited to put an end to historical sanctions and tensions between Iran and USA, through continued interactive diplomatic relations, this was a seminal move after 39 years of hostile relations between Iran and USA.

Republican senators and congressman and Trump entwined to impose economic sanctions and tried to veto the agreement. In the post JCPOA era, Trump began to undermine the credibility of the JCPOA, although UNSG Guterres declared it as a major achievement for Iran's commercial civilization development, as well as military defence structure but furthered international peace and security for the region and the world.

Iran described its nuclear and political logic, and the JCPOA is derived both an international treaty but also under its pragmatic political agreement.

A classic Treaty, works within the framework of the 1969 Vienna, convention, and has to be in written form, governed by international law and is ratified in accordance with articles 7.11.12.13 of the Vienna convention, in various stages – to final ratification, as procedure and signed by attending signatories.

The JCPOA was sealed in accordance with international laws and the Vienna Convention, and once ratified it needed no further process or procedure. Detractors under Trump administration have continued to undermine it post JCPOA era, and wrongly define it as executive political document, which it is not. Resolution 22-31 of UNSC guarantees the implementation of the JCPOA stating it has binding force as law, and all P1+5 nations are obliged under the rule of international laws to implement it in full, whilst also lifting sanctions as per united nations charter.

LEGAL DIPLOMATIC OBLIGATIONS – US IRAN – CONTAINMENT, SYRIA, LEBANON, RUSSIA, USA, APPEASEMENT, ACCEPTANCE OF JURISDICTIONAL STATUS

Iran has legal obligation during its enrichment period for 10 years and IEAE will continue monitoring its R and D and all scientific specifications have been completed in protocols for radioactive uranium safety. All reports are to be filed and stored for Health safety concerns.

Iran managed to annul all economic sanction place on it by the UN and USA.

The sanctions led to a comprehensive lifting of sanctions as multilateral national related to Iran, these were mainly Banking, financial grants, and these were lifted or suspended, while secondary sanctions were removed others were not limiting trade between USA and Iran, the implementation of JCPOA, has overcome restrictions and so moved, the nation to a more positive dynamics as a polity.

The impact on oil and gas sanctions were extremely detrimental for Iran's economy, in oil gas and petrochemical sectors, which has resulted in increased export of oil and gas, in JCPOA post era, shipping, tanker company, have been removed from the sanctions list, again, increasing exports considerably.

Since 2016, Iran has satisfied all its obligations under JCPOA, but no major primary sanctions, were lifted by EU and USA nations, and so bilateral trade has been stifled between these two or three zones.

The new JCPOA has enabled a new horizon for Iran's economy, to emerge Iran is now in a more favourable position and is attracting investment, Europe's dependence on oil imports has increased 90 percent and on gas more than 75%.

IRAN'S MILITARY AS DIPLOMACY REGION SECURITY AND DEFENCE PEACE CONVENTIONS.

Iran maintains its ballistic programmes for defence purposes, only, and new UN resolutions, 2231, article 25 of UN Charter, UNSC resolutions means the annulment of previous and declares Iran's new status is no longer a threat to international peace and security. Iran's foreign policy as new is the result of the JCPOA and Iran's upgraded position and diplomacy has added an international dimension to it. Iran's has become the regional hegemon, for ailing nations in the Arabian Peninsula as Afghanistan, Iraq, Syria, Yemen Lebanon and Palestine and beyond with the international community and UN on their behalf.

The implementation of the JCPOA began on 2016, January and IAEA cemented that all obligations had been implemented but no major sanctions had been lifted by USA, and so the international treaty was partially made ineffective as structure and function, However the post JCPOA era, has made giant leaps towards considerable achievements already good.

DIPLOMACY AND STABILISATION PROCEDURES SUBSTANTIVE AND BY LAWS.

This JCPOA Iran and nations have lifted part of sanctions as has the United Nations, all of the, which is primarily the legal basis through which nations can take the lead and follow suit, otherwise they are not legally permitted to do so. The country's performance has changed indicator comes from various institute reports as well as from the energy security state family of nations, with Iran now I 4th place as energy richest nation, and serial largest gas producer in the world. Iran has since become a member of the BRICS nations ad shares military defence capabilities and cooperation with Russia as it did in Syria and developed with the European union a different legal political ad institutional mind set from the USA, and the different national foreign policy can provide as EU.

For a Strengthening of relations, between them, as well as with the United Nations of the world, as international conglomeration, of nations. The power hegemonic principles and equation has created different components to shift in unilateralistic world order, changing to bilateral and finally multilateralism. The impact of JCPOA has created the positive upward spiral for Iran and the world.

DIPLOMATIC RELATIONS PERSIAN ISLANDS AND EXPANSIVE EMPIRE OF THE EAST.

The foreign policy of Iran under Zafir has greatly improved the standing of Iran, globally and also with the European union, Asia Major and Minor, conglomeration of Indian nation states, China, and far east nations, as well as the Russian federation. Iran has diplomatic relations with the Trans Caucasus and energy diplomacy in the Capsian Sea. Iran has a long relationship with the OIC and nonaligned movement to the GCC (Gulf Cooperation Council) and United Arab Emirates as well as Kuwait. The three islands dispute in the Persian Gulf is being resolved with diplomatic relations between Iran and its allies. Iran has developed fresh allies post joining BRICS and the world strengthening its position in the world. Iran acts as a regional power in the region for only nations and endorses the interim growing council in Iran and urges nations to execute full institutional of Iraq as state power. Iran equally supports Syria post end of its war on Terrorism on 17/12/2017, declaratory by Russia. Iran is involved in the stabilisation of Afghanistan, and its reconstruction as well as the settlement of its refugees. Iran is the main hegemon in the region and is the chief implementer of stabilisation and cooperation with central Asia and the Caucasus and is the political economic power of this region of the Arabian Peninsula and beyond into the international arena, where its superiority and influence is felt among nations as an energy superpower – in oil and as second in the region and gas as first. Iran is equally on its way to becoming a military nuclear power as the largest nation in the region and the most ancient.

There are diplomatic relations ongoing with Iraq with regard to access to Shalt Al Arab waterway. Iran governs the island Arab Tumb or Sughara and great Tumb in the Persian Gulf. The UAE and Iran govern the island Abn Masa since 1992.

The Caspian region between Azerbaijan Iran and Turkmenistan are being resolved, post the breakup of the USSR. Iran's policies post JCPOA have universality and union, descalation of conflicts in the Middle East, encouraging dialogue between ancient civilisations, maintaining an axis of repulsion, to fully protect the rights of Arabian peoples and their fields, oil and gas pipes their natural resources, and their legal nations taken by alien nations as parts and neutral regions, as holy sites. Iran's diplomatic relations with Russia, France, Turkey, Spain, Austria, Netherlands, Italy, Belgium, Sweden, Mexico, Romania, Greece, Brazil, Argentina, Chile, Norway, Switzerland, Afghanistan, Iraq, Saudi Arabia, Eastern Europe, Latin America, and most of the world are good but are suspended with regards to Canada, USA and Yemen. Iran considers African nations as strategic in its portfolio of 20 African nations, and Iran and Ghana, as close and with Libya it has been special since, relations were established, in 1967, when both nations were royal states, ruled by Kings and Queens. South Africa has shared good bilateral relations with Iran since 1994. Canada and Iran severed relations in 1955 when it was under British control in 2012, Canada broke off diplomatic relations with Iran again, but in 2015 Canada sought to repair relations, with Iran, again post JCPOA establishment. Iran and China have developed a strategic partnership and with India, Iran has relations with it for millennia, and with Japan there is a strong strategic relationship with UK, Iran relations have suffered in general when its oil tanker Stena Impero was surrounded and seized by Iranian armed forces, at the strait of Hormuz. However, there is no severance of diplomatic ties. Iran has good relations with Australia and New Zealand.

Iran post JCPOA is a member of BRICS as Russia and allies' nations in peace and conflict, UNESCAP, IAEA, SCO, UNESCO, OPE, UNICTAD, WTO, WHO, WMO, IOC, ISO, and red cross federations. The Academic relations of Iran and United States involve cultural exchange, and between its many universities, Kent, Pennsylvania, Chicago, MIT, Indiana, Utah, Illinois, Alabama, Harvard, Georgetown, State University of New York, and New York Medical college.

DIPLOMACY THE LAWS AND NEGOTIATIONS

JCPOA is the first of a kind under the non-proliferative treaty and has many unique aspects for the first time the UNSC has recognised the nuclear enrichment for a country that is rich in oil and gas, and which is an ancient, developed nation, once a prosperous empire. Several countries have backed it as a major triumph. It was a landmark agreement, in deterring proliferation of nuclear weapons. Some disagreed stating that proliferation in the Arabia peninsula of Arabic nations would come not depending on the details of the agreement, and that nothing will deter Tehran as an oil rich nation to develop itself, to its former glory. IAEA, and USA certified that Iran was complying with the terms of the agreement. President Trump undertook the Iran nuclear agreement review act and soon USA did not recertify the nuclear treaty with Iran, but Theresa May, Emmanuel Macron and Angela Merkel supported the nuclear treaty deal in a joint statement, Federica Mogherini, the EU's policy chief, said the agreement was working efficiently, as EU foreign policy chief and that no single nation could break it unilaterally, made by the UK, France, Germany, Russia, China and EU. Russia confirmed in the positive. However, on 8th of May 2018, USA withdrew from the treaty under President Trump, imposed harsher sanctions on Iran. The US dollars strength went up exponentially. In May 2021, US re-entered negotiations with Iran. In 2023, Iran announced, its rejection of the IAEA, inspectors, and at the 77th session of the UN general assembly Ebrahim Raisa, stated that Iran would never abandon, the pursuant of joy and happiness and civilisation and to do this it would continue to pursue peaceful nuclear energy. In 2023 Israel Palestine war began in Gaza and Anthony Blinken stated that the military aim of the Palestinian Hamas had gone to war, with Israel and Iran was not associated with the attacks. Grossi of IAEA kept on prioritising Iran's safeguard agreement, but rejection of inspection was deemed in appropriate and unprecedented.

DIPLOMACY PERSIAN CULTURAL CIVILIZATIONAL DEVELOPMENT IN IRAN.

The foreign diplomacy changed under the Obama administration and Iran became a new focus with John Kerry. Political and economic pressures were placed on Iran due to the ability of Iran, to develop its nuclear capacities for military and civilizational purposes. Hassan Rouhani was the head of Iran and Javid Zarif was the foreign under and the nuclear negotiations began. Six nations took part in the negotiations, and Iran presented its model, this enables Iran to transit to peaceful nuclear capacity. The agreement JCPOA was reached on 14 July 2015 and ended arguments over its transition at the UN security council.

President Trump and his administration were against the JCPOA ever having been formulated, they took positive steps against it and began to reduce its validity in multiple ways, it did not end there, they began to impose active and egregious sanctions as new against Iran and then step by step began to limit the JCPOA, the spirit and the letter of the laws of the agreement were nullified, and the multilateral agreement (UN resolution 2231 UNSC) to one between the USA and Iran but also EU was unilaterally by the USA was annulled, but the EU tried to defend the treaty JCPOA, through foreign relations departments and teams and equally under the International laws, it had been composed, hence their legal teams, but to no avail, and a division of the two nation states USA and EU was created.

Normalisation of ties had begun with Hassan Rouhani, a constructive collaboration discourse Even with confrontation, interactive discourse, to shift foreign policy of the 11th government of Iran. The integration of European nations ad USA had begun to coverage with little relative divergence, albeit different stances and positions were debated.

First debate as Diplomacy the success was arriving at an agreement with the JCPOA with many institutions and key public officers of multiple nations.

II DIPLOMACY IRAN ARABIAN PENINSULA AND PARTNERSHIPS SYRIA

Iran's involvement in Syria, along with co-partners Lebanon, Syria, Russia – analysis of Iran's foreign diplomatic policy in Peace and Conflict, in the Arabian Peninsula.

This chapter explores Iran's involvement in the Arabian Peninsula with a particular emphasis on Iran's involvement in the Arabian Peninsula in the Syrian war since 2011. Iran's geopolitical economic, commercial and strategic interests in Syria, Iran's impact on Syria, its intervention with co-partners mainly Syria, as nation and Lebanon as well as Russia an ally of Iran, in the BRICS conglomeration of nations, which rose as regional influence, to protect Syria, from collapse, from the fall out of Iraq's and Libya's armies and terror groups such as AL-Qaeda, AL Nusra and others. Iran got busy protecting ports countering USA and allies' dominance in the region. Military, economic, diplomatic activities of Iran's involvement are analysed including Iran and BRICS nations, mainly Russia's portrayal of its involvement in the rescue of Damascus Syria. This chapter underscores, the consequences of Iran's and Russia's intervention and evaluate international relations to BRICS and Iran offering insights into Iran's complex role with her partners in Arabia and resulting in global consequences. The comprehensive understanding of Iran's involvement in Syria impacted it negatively. Iran is the sole Arabian nation that emerged as a key participant with geopolitical interests in rescuing Syria but mainly Damascus from collapsing. Other international allies such as Russia, China, Lebanon, also played crucial roles of particular note is the involvement alongside Iran and Syria was Russia.

This situation required USA to further its geopolitical ambition and protect its assets and interests across the region. Iran, BRICS, Lebanon, Russia's interest in Syria, is investigated by Iran's centuries long engagement in Arabia, from its imperial time, till today, Iran's unique interplay of geography strategy tactics in Syria, has reshaped her foreign policy in Arabia, with Arabian nations. Iran's active role in Arabian conflict from

Arab Israeli, disputes to Iran Iraq wars, where its involvement played an important role in maintaining the balance of power, in the region. Various effects of Arab unrest, show its influence, as donning economic challenges and exacerbating crisis after crisis.

IRAN ARABIAN STATE OF DIPLOMACY

Diplomacy papers explore all the knowledge in Iran, and Russia's involvement in Syria, in 2011, and exiting in 2017.

Iran's unwavering support for Assad government sovereignty of Syria underpins Iran and Russia's domestic politics. Russia, Iran, Syria, ties are a policy to prevent Syria from becoming another unstable nation, causing further regional instability.

Russia deployed military into Syria along with Iran and thus this began a vital tool for diplomacy.

With Iran and this began a vital tool for diplomacy, in this region, Syria is a geopolitically strong operational base geographically and strategically thus activating and engaging many players as France, Lebanon, UK, USA, Russia and Iran. Russia Iran's interests in Syria, altered the balance of power, helped, Assad to prevent the fall of Syria, Russia, Iran, Syria's economic strategic objectives became strengthened, Russian Iran, Syria, policy goals, were fulfilled and equally improved Russia's relations with other regional and global powers mainly Turkey, Iran, Afghanistan, in the region.

SYRIA'S CONFLICT WITH IRAN AND RUSSIA'S INVOLVEMENT.

Iran's and Russia's involvement in Syria had implications for regional and global security and influenced broader geopolitics across, the entire region, and worldwide.

Iran Russia's participation in the Syrian conflict provides how international relations, geopolitics and foreign policies changed worldwide. Diplomatic frameworks were altered as theory and practice. Dualism is approaching good nations use as platonic to international relations since the formulation of the Artha shastra, the first diplomatic treatise created in Sanskrit in greater India, under its then emperors and used by them to harmonise, their nations. The role of power and self-interests plays a minor role as state behaviour. The Noble state acts to secure the security and sovereignty of a nation by the use of just military and economic power, if needed. It is within the framework that Iran and Russia's objective were achieved in Syria.

Russia, Iran geopolitics – in diplomacy in Syria exposed how the terrain of Syria interacted with politics and diplomacy as the geography of Syria and Arabia, shapes behaviour and local ties. Strategic location plays a part too. Iran's approach emphasized its role in shaping territorial boundaries, and structuring Syria's overall foreign policy goals. Iran's use of construction influenced the collaboration's behaviour emphasising ideas and norms over merely state power, and national interests, reshaping domestic norms and international concepts.

Russia emphasised the role of diplomacy in reshaping Syria and arresting her security threats. Iran, stressed the role of economic relationships, arming nations, revising inequality and under development of key states in the region, and in conflict resolution and wider regional issues.

International law dictates the framework, and the legal norms regulate international diplomatic relations, Iran used these as an enhanced political theory and Russia emphasised that right market forces contribute to stability and so development and growth. Iran in Syria concentrated on key arguments, on the legal basis of the complex dynamics of Syria's conflict and Russia helped uncover many dynamic drivers causing and accelerating the fall of Damascus in Syria.

IRAN ARABIAN PROCEDURAL SUBSTANTIVE DIPLOMACY

Iran utilized guidelines for conducting its diplomacy and geopolitical actions, its objectives were to alter policy, paradigms, curbing realistic and idealist approaches. Iran understood more than most, and also the relevance of Russia's involvement impact, focus on language, and to stifle, using propaganda, to stabilise Syria from imminent collapse.

IRAN ARABIAN LIMITATION OF DIPLOMACY

Iran used rigorous methods with some drawbacks as not a completely meticulous approach, but effective. The entry created fractious relationships with Europeans especially UK, EU, France and USA. Russia and Iran deployed alternative means to arrest the flow of ISIS, ISIL, AQ, AL Qaeda in Syria.

The shortenings of Iran were overcome by Russian assessment, policy and intelligence information. Together, the geopolitical goals in Syria were achieved through a clear comprehensive understanding.

THE PERSIA EMPIRE AS DIPLOMACY RUSSIA AND SYRIA.

Iran and Russia interest in Syria goes back to the times of the Persian and Russian empires. In the 18th 19th centuries, their influence reached as far as the Black Sea, Mediterranean, and trade routes, between various ports. The empires often got embroiled in conflicts with the Turkish Ottoman empire and these impacted relations between the trade powers as a whole.

Russia clashed with Persia as well and the two fought battles in the Caucasus region and regions of Azerbaijan and parts of Iran. Russia often controlled Constantinople Bosphorus Strait to get greater access to the Mediterranean and it allied with France, Britain during world war I and tried to curb the expansionist model of the Ottoman empire and in the Middle East. The region played a pivot role and after the Russian revolution, Russia formed strong relations with Arabian nations, and which became independent post world wars, especially Egypt, Syria, and Iraq. Russia provided economic and military aid, and this region shaped both USA ad Russia ideologies and Nasir and others exerted influence. With the coming of Vladimir Putin, Russia became dominant again in the Arabian Peninsula. The relations thus go back to before world wars, and despite the dissolution of the Soviet Union. Russia's strategic partnerships, with Syria, Iran grew, over time, and these others countered western influence there. Russian companies began to provide expertise in the oil and gas zones of Syria. The tension with NATO consolidated relations with Syria and a complex web of allies created a profound shift in Syria and Iran relations, and important developments began and Syria's policy with Arabian nations began to change rapidly.

DIPLOMACY AND ECONOMIC HISTORIES.

Syria went through different stresses due to the wars in Iraq, Libya. Operations in nearby Iraq, Libya, and operations nearby Palestine, these contributed greatly to political and economic competitions which were exacerbated by civil unrest in the country but also some rogue groups and fallen armies circulating in the region. The most prominent economic development was to exploit its oil and gas reserves to create a society of wealthy and politically well-connected businessmen and women,

Syria economic history achieved major economic progress, and it was heavily dependent on energy markets, oil and gas production which fed its other sectors, like textiles, food processing and banking sectors. Syria was a naturally rich complex landscape and political pluralism thrived. Syria is comprised mainly of Sunni Muslims, with other minor minorities. The Alawites have always been in control. Political reform began with the introduction of legislation for elections and decentralizing administrative powers. Syria maintained close ties with Iran and Russia, with Turkey and Lebanon. Overall Syria's development is marked with economic challenges to develop its oil and gas fields, Iran and Russia have sought.

DIPLOMACY AND EGALITARIANISM

Iran and Russia's interest in Syria was purely egalitarian, to rescue Syria, to prevent its collapse, being a strong ally of Syria, and it sought to stand close to Syria in its crisis. Vladimir Putin and Assad held numerous meetings as well as with Iran to discuss regional issues and developments paving a way to discuss ways of securing the nation and both became involved in Syria, communications were crucial to avoid unintended collisions with America operating in Iraq and to coordinate safe actions. Israel was viewed by Assad as an existential threat to its sovereignty invading its airspace launching strikes against its allies. Russia, Iran and Lebanon, and disturbing their geopolitical aims to stabilise Syria and the region. The parts of importance in Syria, were as drivers to curb instability and violence in Syria, and to prevent disturbances, from Palestine Israel, factors to enter the country. The Syria, unrest played a fundamental reason for influencing changes in the Arabia peninsula. Russia Iran tried to act as mediators between Syria and the Arabia to restore differences between them, and to create better relations as negotiation for stability in the region. Iran and Russia's role in the Syria conflict, can be viewed by their strategic goals for stability in the region, by developing relation with ai nations, Lebanon, Iran and Syria. The dynamics during the war led to a greater formation of a network excluding Israel as the antagonist and enforcing relations with a wider nation in the Arabian Peninsula. Iran, Russia, Lebanon, played as instrumental role, in Syria and Iraq, since the Iran-Iraq war from 1980 to 1988. Russia shifted towards Iran and away from Iraq, to maintain equilibrium and stability in the Arabian Peninsula. The decision to do was mainly to maintain stability as a stratagem interest for Russia and curb US hegemonic influence as eroding over time. Moscow still considers Iraq as ally and preserves relations with it as well as Ira, Syria, Lebanon, and assists it with advisers political and military. Iran tries to maintain the balance of power in the world with Russia by converting USA and allies often Malin fluence, in the Arabian Peninsula and thus brings into the fray all Arabian nations to align with the world balance of power shopping the American one in the region, this it has done successfully. Syria and Iran, Iraq, Lebanon, are closely aligned, due to shared ideologies and the war of decades in the peninsula.

US, however, has a stronghold over Iraq, since the Iraq war and so Syria asked for Russian Iranian and Lebanese support. The aid Iran, Russia gave to bolster Syria's position is complex and multidimensional considering all political, social, economic elements into their working paradigms. The fallen armies of Iraq, Libya as ISIS, ISIL, made their inroads into Syria, and terror groups from the Afghan, African, regions, flooded, into Syria, which became a melting pot, had a significant repercussions for Syria, it became, vulnerable like Iraq, following US invasion in 2003, and creating the armies, as fallen and organised as ISIS and ISIL, and extremist terror groups established themselves as AQ and Al Nusra, they spread across Iraq

Syria, Libya, and which implicated all three zones, creating ramifications across borders. ISIS was formed by the Iraq war as a survival strategy against the USA and the borders of Iraq, Syria, became porous. ISIS and ISIL moved their soldiers and fighters as a Caliphate with armoured jeeps, weapons and resources. Syria was besieged and an intense drought worsened conditions with struggling agricultural centres. Peace protests were brokered by talks in Geneva which were run by the UN and included the Arab League, to create a ceasefire with Iraq formed ISIS and Libya formed ISIL but there was no cessation of hostilities.

The unrest from eastern and north African countries into Syria, in 2011, spread outwards from Tunisia and into the Arab nations. This wave arrived in Syria, and Syria tried to stop the infiltration and in flux but failed. The North African nations revolt came from sectarian conflicts, and it had a negative impact on Syria's humanitarian status. Syrians departed abroad and UNHCR reordered that they had been displaced to Turkey, Lebanon, Jordan, Iraq, Egypt and Europe. The Caliphates, Iraqi, Libya, Muslim states were in all three countries after Iraq, Libya a war, Syria, too. The fallen soldiers became fighters and tried to protect Syria from invading forces, but clashed with each other, being from different nations, Civil opposition came from Islamists groups, such as the Muslim brotherhood, Free Syrian army (FSA) Syrian national Council (SNC) Kurdish groups.

DIPLOMACY EVOLVING ROLES OF HEZBOLLAH, IRAN, RUSSIAN, TURKEY

At first, Turkey focused on the Kurds, but Russia, backed Syria, extensively along with Iran, UK, France, also intervened in Syria.

Russia, Syria, Iran helped to reconstruct Syria, and helped Syria to preserve its commercial alliances, whilst also developing Syria's oil fields, her transportation, nations power, plants, and Russian, Iranian, firms flooded into the region, Syria is at the crossroads, of Key energy routes, and Russia, Iran, helped Syria meet its energy goals.

DIPLOMATIC POLICIES STRATEGY AND TACTICS.

Syria its interest and goals are related and its motivations stem from these two gains. Its core needs are its nations to protect and achieve stability, by reducing threats, and increasing strategic opportunities, whilst maintaining territorial integrity.

Syria's objectives, actions decisions were attained by planning tangible outcomes, precise and measurable with Russia and Iran as key allies. Border concerns were to fuel and further these interests. Russia Iranian rescue in Syria was national and security-based interest. Russia Iranian military intervention in Syria were timely and sharpened regional and global dynamics. Iran's operation was to advance Syria's interests in the region and to help it formulate a better foreign policy, with these both internal and external developments saw dramatic shifts. Their success increased their status in the world, in ways that could not be comprehended. Russia, Iran, together changed the balance of power in the world, with its allies to one side versus Russia and allies on the other. Russia looked after the Tartus naval station, secured it, and Iran reshaped the unipolar world order.

DIPLOMATIC INITIATIVES AND GOVERNANCE

Iran's diplomatic efforts with Russia were aligned to secure it, both worked to strengthen Syria and projected its image, responsibility and sought peace initiatives with Astana Process.

Both nations were driven by strategic and regional constitutions. Russia and Iran's state-owned energy companies, expressed an interest to develop Syria's energy sector and to help with its infrastructure development projects. Iran expressed interest to extracting Syria's mineral resources phosphate mining agreements, were signed. Iran's operation in Syria, came under considerable criticism, but Russia, aided Iran to shift the government of Assad, and they gained back control of key areas of Syria. Syria's security objectives were met by both Russia and Iran connecting their power into the Mediterranean region.

Iran and Russia rivalries were played in Syria. Iran, Russia took certain points to direct diplomatic channels with fighting parties in Astana, de-escalation zones, were set up by Iran, across the country to decrease violence and humanitarian help and preserve exchanges were discussed. Syria's future political structure governance regions and revisions. Dialogue was opened up between Syrian government opposition organisations. Sochi conference bought the realisation of these strategic goals together Russia Iran's involvement in Syria brought the four nations, together including Lebanon and Turkey. Cultural diplomacy was enhanced between the nations, and cross-cultural discussions to preserve heritage and restoration of the culture.

Overall Iran and Russia's involvement in Syria disturbed regional balances, putting US and allies out of the key conflict, and long-term recovery for Syria began. American invasion of Iraq in 2003, caused debate due to miscalculation of mass destruction on weapons, but Iran and Syria were united for Syria united Syria to save its fall and to end terrorism in the region.

China welcomed Russia's interventionism in Syria and so BRICS a conglomeration of Nations were set up. Russia, Iran Syria jointly declared the end of the wars on terrorism having defeated ISIS and ISIL and terror groups on the 17th of December 2017. Soldiers surrendered their arms of both ISIS and ISIL and submitted to Russia's conversion doctrine. Iran's involvement in Syria had an enormous influence on its relationship with Turkey and an advantageous cooperation and relationship was cemented despite obstacles. Syria has served to illustrate that a nation can be saved by robust and strong allies that favour its sovereignty from rogue forces. Iran's aim to restore governance, structure, encourage social and economic development are of parts of its aims for the long-term stability and recovery.

III DIPLOMATIC PARALLELS TO EASTERN EUROPE AND WEST

Alexis de Tocqueville made a prophecy, a the 1830' that there would always be two great people or nations who from different points of departure will advance to the same end – Russia and America. The circumstances out of which the cold war arose are simple enough to outlie. The Traditional boundary of the Russia empire extended from the eastern Baltic to the black sea. To the west of the boundary were buffer states (Finland, Estonia, Lithuania, Poland and the Balkans)

To the western side of these buffer states lay Germany, Austria, Italy and France. Historically, the enormous power of Russia had been contained or balanced by other powers that were European.

The principal power was Germany, but the elements of equilibrium were lost after 1945, when World War II ended. The Soviet Union it seemed by the sleight of hand, had swallowed up half of Europe, and Moscow had stamped its authority on a line that ran through the middle of Europe north to South (Levering 1982,). The action of Moscow it seemed was a reflection of its past historic experiences. The polarisation of the world between two powers was not accidental product of accidental circumstances. The birth of Karl Marx in Germany and the entrance of a revolutionary changed Russia and substituted the Czarist regime. The implications of this are essential to the understanding of the cold war. The behaviour of the Russian under the communists has been Russian behaviour rather than communist. Communist Russia continued to behave essentially as it behaved under the Czars. The same centralisation, authoritarians, conspiratorial behaviour, In international relations, the same distrust of the outsider world.

The obsession with secrecy and espionage increased with the revolution in 1917, and the same effort to achieve security by expanding the Russian space, by constantly pushing back the menacing presence of the foreigners across the Russian borders (Halle 1958).

The American strategies was the opposite of that of the Russian, unlike the Russians who had always been aware of their weakness and pending dangers, the Americas had been aware of their strength and lack of danger. The Americas had learnt the lesson of world war I, but if the other European countries had learned to act with wisdom, all subsequent disasters could have been averted; the economic collapse of the 1930's, the failure of Germany's republic, and the rise of Hitler. However, like all things everything conspired and hard lessons had to be learnt again, in World War II. However, the understanding of the realities was still to be grasped, and the seeds of the cold war were sown (Albert 1959, Keylor 2012). In 1945, there was a new creation of power vacuum on either side of Russia into which it expanded. There is no reason to take it for granted that what happened In Europe, In the three years after the war was, and all its features, the realization of plans with which Stalin had anticipated the opportunities that victory would bring. His aims intentions were to establish, the most defensible frontiers that Moscow could control. However, the dynamics of what happened in Europe was essentially determined by the vacuum of power in Europe and it was regenerated. When Russia tried to affect a limited disengagement in Austria, Poland and Hungary, it produced the uprising of 1956, a political earthquake and what happened in Poland, Czechoslovakia shook the very seat of power in Moscow. By the closing days of the war, a series of decisions, on post war settlement were made by the three leaders of the coalition against Hitler. From Washington point of view, other problems were more important that of post war, international organisation, the success, of which would pave the way for solution of all other problems. The realisation of the plans for the United Nations organisation, was to take precedent over such particular issues as that of the future of Poland. At the Yalta conference, 1945, Churchill, and Roosevelt both wanted the establishment of Poland. Beginning with the new Year, there were two governments of Poland, were recognised by Whitehall and Washington the others by Moscow.

A formula was agreed, for their right to self-determination, by free elections and a disagreement foreshadowed the cold war, with Russia extended, to include the whole of Poland, while resentment and alarm grew in the west. The fall of Romania, Hungary, Bulgaria, and Czechoslovakia into Russia hands fell soon after. Where the walls the surround a power go down the result may be disaster to only for its neighbours, but also for the power itself. At the end of the war, many countries suffered economic hardships, France and Italy floundered. It was this that drew America back to the continent. The collapse of Hitler's might occur in the first week of May 1945. America which then saw the spread of its power, over the pacific and eastern Asia was in disarray. President Truman then took the decision to use the atomic bomb. On August 6th, 1945, the first of the new atomic bombs obliterated Hiroshima and, on the August 8, Nagasaki was obliterated. Japan decided to surrender, and officially World War II was over on August 14th in the same year. America was in search of an efficient foreign policy devised the Marshall Plan and entered into negotiations, with other nations; Moscow was surprised and chose to resist the Marshall plan. However, there was the success of the European recovery program in spite of Moscow's opposition. In reaction to the Marshall plan, the Russians created the Cominform (to provide economic support for the easter bloc countries), and a return to the conscription in the United States and the conclusion of the Brussels pact (between the European powers) and the formation of the western EU.

The reaction to the belief of the America leaders were creating a capitalist world and the destruction of the soviet state was unbearable. The Marxists ad Leninists philosophy was expounded. For the Russians the Truman doctrine and Marshall plan showed that a new assault was in preparation. The Russian retaliation was with equal measure before the Warsaw pact. Once the cold war was established countries aligned with one power or the other and some but very few were truly aligned. The Warsaw pact a mutual defence treaty between eight county states, signed in 1955 was operational till the fall of the cold war, under Gorbachev, in 1991 (Keylor 2012, ye, 2012, Hopkins 2007, Luke 2012). There were many intense phases of the cold war which culminated in many conflicts and crisis as well as international incidents, the chief being the berlin blockade (1948-1940, the Korean war (1950-53), Berlin crisis of 1965, and other international incidents such as the downing of the Korean airlines in 1983, under Kennedy, and Khrushchev administration raised oral issues, when the world almost stumbled to the brink of the cliff (Levering

1982, Roberts 2006, ye 2012, Keylor 2012). In ideological terms, the cold war presented itself as a worldwide contest between liberal democrats and the communists. The formulations were mythical, like the Berlin Blockade, and its failure, with the Berlin Blockade, the conflict between Russia and the west fatally crossed the lines of diplomatic niceties and took on what resembles a war. America expanded its power into the defence of west Europe, and which could not be made with each country working separately. After urgent requirements for economic rehabilitation, made by the Marshall Plan, the organisation of the western defence was top priority. This resulted in the formation of NATO, and later attacks across the lines, separated the two sides as Europe and the Balkans, the Middle east and the eastern nations of Russia, China, India as Asia Major and Asia Minor. The far eastern policy of the United States created many crises in the 1950's. Surprise attacks in Korea resulted in the improvisation by USA to meet it. Shortly one after another countries began to defect, like Yugoslavia, and at the same time, the arms race began in earnest escalating the cold war between countries of the west and the east. The Korean War, was seen as a western success, provoked by Chinese intervention. The chief feature of the cold war was to be the arms race, both sides appeared to be advancing towards a final clash, which would be set off by an accidental event and decisions of both sides.

The arguments that were made that the military undertaking represented by NATO, was necessary that it could only intensify the cold war by giving more provocation. (Keylor 2012). The thesis thus posited was the Russian expansionism is what triggered the cold war, this is the traditional view held by the majority of evidence of events, however there are revisionists, that point that America triggered it, and still post revisionists feel that power vacuums resulted in the weakness of structure and thus bipolarity came into existence, with the crash of the Berlin wall, economic distress in Russia, created a domino effect, and many states fell under Russian control, then fell out, one by one, by one, and then later Soviet union ceased to exist.

DIPLOMATIC PARADIGMS IRAN AND RUSSIA

Since 2014, the change in the ideational paradigms in the Middle east, arrived in the form of civil unrest and Russia – the Syrian civil war had become a multisided conflict, with Syria, Russia Iran, the Baathist Syrian party, the Arab republic led by President Bashar Al Assad, and other domestic allies, and various foreign forces, i.e. USA, UK, EU, Israel, Australia, Canada, New Zealand, opposing both the Syrian government and each other to different degrees and in various spheres via different strategies, tactics and combinations that were innovative, novel and never used by traditional warfare. The initial paradigm did not involve, Iran and Russia but was unilaterally dictated by USA and her allies in the region, including, Syria opposition parties. However, the breakdown products of many nations were in Syria, Iraq, Libya, Palestine, Nigeria, Egypt and Africa nations. Thus, the classic balance of power doctrine was not operating and became functional only through the entry of Russia, into the fray of the civil war of Syria in the Middle east. The civil war in Syria, was part of the wider wave of Arab unrest, a conflict spilling over from the wars, in Libya, Iraq, Gaza – Palestine, Afghanistan, Yemen, and other parts of Africa, other eastern, and central. The Arab Spring erupted all over the Africa, Arab continent and spilled over and consolidated the war in Syria in 2013.

The Africa Arabia nations, gelled as one, especially the conflict zones and spilling in from Egypt, Libya, eastern, western and central Africa, as well as other conflicts in the middle east from 2011 – 2019 i.e., Iraq, Palestine, Israel and Yemen. Iran knew that the Syrian war was a combination of factors spills from Iraq, Palestine, and Libya, and the rest of the Arab African spring, factions, in Syria that were disconnected with the Syria government, and their collection of groups, that called for regime change and the removal of Assad as president. Thus, amidst the chaos, of the middle east conflicts, a new wave of unrest began, and the Assad government moved quickly to contain the unrest such that the Syrian government and the state of Syria would not collapse and fail. The many sides engaged in Syria's conflict, were, Iran Russia and her allies, and USA, UK, and her allies, held different perspectives about the Syrian war, as well as the Civil war, since the end of the wars of Libya, and Iraq. Palestine operations since 2014, developed different points of view, stances, paradigms and justifications to support their sides. The Syrian war was particularly violent, the factions, marched to Damascus, and Aleppo, and various violent tribes, factions, and groups had fallen armies of Iraq and Libya in them as well as terror groups began to fight with each other and against Assad as well as the factions as groups.

The Syrian army began to flounder in the face of such organised and a well-developed assault, by armies of factions, the Sunni opposition, terror, groups, the free Syrian army Salafists, Jihadists, the Al Nusra front, the mixed Kurdish Arabs, Saudi groups, Shia groups, and the Syrian democratic forces, and the fallen armies of Iraq and the fallen armies of Libya, also ISIS and ISIL with various countries, in the region that supported the factions, armed groups either directly or indirectly with arms, ammunitions, and supplies. Diplomatic frays and doctrines paradigms shattered 100 moves. With the USA and allies who held a seminal argument, about regime change, latterly Russia, activated, the cold war balance of power doctrine, and instituted a novel paradigm, of containment by conversion of radical groups of civil unrest in Syria and reasserting its doctrine of the right to protect.

IRAN RUSSIA SYRIA MIDDLE EAST, ARABIA DIPLOMACY

Iran and Russia formed forces with Assad's government and thus prevented the fall of Damascus and Aleppo primarily and it proclaimed this via its diplomatic venues, MFA, Russia on public channels such as e-diplomacy on the internet and cyberspace, as well as by its officially released documents in December 2017. So how did this all come about, what were the key events that wrung in changes to the entrenched Middle East paradigms since 2001.

Iran and Russia loosely connected with BRICS, (Brazil, India, China and South Africa), after it was ousted from the G8 nations ad strongly connected with Syria and Iran, Hezbollah in Lebanon. It then entered the fray to support, the Syrian Arab republic government and Assad and spilled over and culminated in the Arab spring, in Syria in the year 2011. The Arab Spring movement, constitutional members, from all over Arabia, especially, the conflict zones and equally spilling in from Egypt, Libya, eastern, western, and central Africa, as well as other conflicts, in the middle east, from 2011 – 2019, i.e., Iraq, Palestine Israel and Yemen.

The Syria Arab spring claimed they were discontented, with the Syrian Government, and their collection of groups, demanded regime change and called for the removal of Assad as President. Thus, amidst the chaos of the Middle east, conflicts, a new wave of unrest began, and the Assad government, moved quickly to contain the unrest, such that Syria's government and the state of Syria, would not collapse and fall. Iran did everything to prevent this.

The two sides engaged in Syria's conflict mainly, Iran, Russia and her allies, and US, UK and her allies held different perspectives about the Syrian civil war, since 2014, as the evolving situation warranted, and each side, developed different viewpoints stances, paradigms, justifications, to support their political opinions.

The civil war was particularly suppressed, until the unrest marched into the capital of Syria, which is Damascus, and Aleppo, and various violent tribes, factions and groups, melted into the Arab spring, and began to fight within these regions against Assad, and against each other. The Syrian army began to flounder in the face of such organised and well developed assault by armed factions – the Sunni opposition rebel groups, the freedom of the Syrian army, Salafi Jihadist groups, the Nusra front, the mixed Kurdish Arabia, Saudi Arab groups, Sunni militia groups, Syrians democratic forces and the Islamic state of Iraq and Islamic state of the Levant, with various prominent countries, in the region supporting the factions and armed groups, either directly or indirectly with arms, ammunition, money and supplies. Several armies entered the fray, with the

USA and allies who held a seminal argument about regime change, latterly Russia, activated the cold war balance of power doctrine and instituted a novel paradigm of containment by conversion of radical groups of civil unrest, in Syria and reasserting the doctrine of right to protect. Iran and Russia formed forces with Assad's government and thus prevented the fall of Damascus and Aleppo, primarily and it proclaimed this with its diplomatic venues MFA Russia on public channels such as e-diplomacy twitter on the internet and cyber space as well as by its officially released documents in December 2017. So how did this all come about, what were the key events, that wrung in changes to the entrenched Middle East paradigms since 2001.

DIPLOMACY IRAN AND THE FORMATION OF BRICS

Iran and Russia loosely connected with BRICS, Brazil, India, China and South Africa, after it was ousted from the G8 nations, of which it was once a part, and which was officially reduced to G7 nations and strongly connected with Syria and Iran, Hezbollah in Lebanon. It then entered the fray to support the Syrian Arab republic, government and Assad, and the Syria Armed forces militarily, as they were about to collapse in Damascus and Aleppo, due to the growing strength of the anti-regime forces. Iran and Russia began to conduct airstrikes, and other strategic military operations, in September 2015, and the USA led international coalition, in Syria since 2015 shifted its stance from the removal of Assad and his regime. Under Obama and Kerry administration, a shift of foreign policy was declared and refocused on countering ISIL, and an open declaration of this policy, was made, once Russia, began supporting the Syrian government. USA led force conducted airstrikes against ISIL, with Arab nations, and with western allies, but equally government and pro-government areas were accidentally hit. Special forces, artillery, units were sent into Syria to counter ISIL, by Anglo American governments. The US perspective and dynamic was from the start dramatically opposed to Russia and both sides openly vociferously supported their agenda with the US supporting the democratic federation of Northern Syria, and its armed wing SDF and the Syrian militia armed forces, through military support, finances, and personnel and with trainers in logistics. Russia held a diametrically opposed view to the US and endorsed Syria under the right to protect doctrine and principle. Turkey equally, engaged actively, with the Syrian opposition, which with its support, began to occupy large swathes of northwestern Syria, whilst still engaging significant ground fought through battles, against ISIL, SDF, Syrian democratic forces, and its newly formed DPNS structures.

DIPLOMACY IRAN RUSSIA AND NATO EXPANSIONISM

Between the years, 2011 – 2019, the fighting from the Syria civil war began to create anomalies, in the region including Lebanon and Iraq - ISIL and Al Nusra began to fight with DPNS against the Lebanon's army, Israel too conducted several military campaigns, against Syria and her allies, Lebanon, Hezbollah, and the Iranian forces based on the ground and from the air.

Thus, like the forty-year cold wars, held in proxy nations in the Far East, mainly the oriental world, post-World War II Syria became the battleground for a renewed cold war, between Russia and her allies and USA and her allies. Other nations began to be gradually drawn in, such as Turkey, Qatar, Saudi Arabia, Egypt, Jordan and Lebanon. Turkey became extremely agitated and became deeply entrenched in her petition, against the Syrian government, actively participating, in airstrikes, against ISIL as part of NATO alongside the USA led coalition.

The United Nations, intervened, positively to quell the cruel unrest, but equally to prevent the conflict escalating, between USA allies and Russian led allies. International organisations too began to become active, as the civil war mutated into extreme and unusual forms, with the USA and allies and Russia and allies' positions, hardening and getting more entrenched.

Massacres, violence, were common, as the conflict involved groups and particularly the entire world. Refugees in their thousands and millions began to stream out of Syria Several emerging peace initiatives had to be launched, as the conflicts raged on and both Astana (Russia led) and Geneva (USA led) talks began on Syria and the United nations, being the arbiter between two strongly held views, diagrammatically opposed in an extreme sense – with the US supporting the paradigm and principle of sovereignty of Syria as paramount and the Nation's right to protect its integrity at all times – the right to protect doctrine stemming from the sovereign rights of the State and based on statehood principles and jurisprudence and Russia reasserted that President Assad was head of Syria's legitimate government. 2017 saw an escalation in peace talks held both by Russians in Astana and the Americans in Geneva. It is well known through politico historical records that the Baath government only came to power post Syria's independence in 1963.President Hafez Al-Assad, an Alawite became the first president of Syria, with a republican constitution. President Basar – AL Assad became the President on the death of his father in 2000. The twin towers fell in 2001 and the wars in the Middle east commenced shortly after beginning with Iraq. Post the 2011, civil war supported by USA and allies, a multiparty election, was held and the people's council of Syria, instituted their President. Assad's father was the one who on the 31st of January 1973 instituted a running constitution for Syria. It opened the way, unlike prior frugal constitutions to remove the mandatory operation that the President of Syria had to be a Muslim. This increased the opposition by Muslims in the region, and strikes began in Homs, Hama, Aleppo and Latakia. The four corridors of Euphrates opened up and around Damascus, a coup was organised by the Muslims in various factions and groups, including the Muslim brotherhood and associated groups. Earlier too, historically the same government was under siege as early as 1976 to 1982, and armed revolts by Islamic fundamentalist groups were growing pace, in this period of Syria's history. Upon his father's death, Assad and his wife, Asma, a Sunni Muslim born and educated in London rose, to serve Syria and wrung in several democratic reforms.

Critics and commentators gave him no credit in aspiring to do so. Thus, the history of opposition, by former Islamic groups of 1976-1982, grew again but with much more violent vigour, to remove him from office, but also supported by domestic Arab nations, and foreign nations. Syria, by now was composed of many ethnic groups, Arab, Alawite, Kurd, and Levantine – several sects of Muslims, Sunni Alawite and Shia. Christians and Jews are recent entries. Syria's GDP increased, compared to other Arab nations and sub-Saharan nations under the Assad successive government. However, unemployment rates began to increase, since as early as 2009 and several cities reported poverty rates, such as Dara and Homs. Syria faced intense drought since 2006 – 2011, widespread crop failures, increase in food prices, and failed infrastructure, which were not mitigated by the spill over from the Iraq and Libyan wars, of over 2.5 million refugees and more forming every year. The war has a curious timeline beginning in March 2011, with a sudden insurgency in April 2012, an attempted ceasefire by the UN in May 2013 and further escalations witnessed from 2012-2013. Islamist groups began to infiltrate in record numbers from January to September 2014 and USA led interpretation began in southern Syria in 2015 and spread to Northwestern Syria, Idlib, Palmyra, Al-Hasakah and river regions.

Russian intervention began seriously in September 2015, with partial ceasefires. Aleppo was recaptured by the Syrian governments by the Russia and allies, in December 2016 and a partial ceasefire was declared an interim interval.

IRAN DIPLOMACY – ESCALATION ZONES SYRIA ZONES AND RIVERS.

Several de-escalation zones, were constructed between April and July 2017, following the Khan Shaykhum chemical attack, the Shayrat strikes, Hama offensive and other minor upsets, Russia moved in vigorously after Aleppo and broke the siege of Dier -al -Zour from the region, and Russia became permanently stationed there. The Iranian and Russian armies advanced in Hama province and Ghouta and the Turks tried to intervene in Afrin in March 2018, which resulted in further Syrian campaigns from October 2018 to February 2019, against Turkish military operation in Afrin, resulting in Rif Dimashq offensive and the Israel Syria offensive in 2018/2019. Finally, the Dama chemical attack, surfaced in southern Syria, followed by additional; US led missile strikes and the southern Syria offensive in August 2018. Under the new Trump administration, Idlib province, demilitarisation was announced, and the withdrawal of troops, with Iraq entering the fray from September 2018, against ISIL targets in Syria. Russian forces became a permanent presence in Syria, backed by the Assad government. However, the ISIL, attacks continued unabated from January 2019, to present. The belligerents and various factions both foreign and domestic – ISIL, the Turkish backed Syria, free army, Christian militias from UK and Europe manifested in the Syrian civil war, CIA operations, US special operation troops, began training the army of the SDF and thousands of rebel opposition groups and forces in Syria, activated the operations beginning as early as 2012 but lasting till the present, in spite of intervention by Russia, Iran and Syria. The international community reacted vociferously as did the Arab league, European Union and the United Nations. But there was no conclusion, and the skirmishes went on unabated although the majority, were quelled by the Russians and Syria and USA and its allies too acted against ISIS and ISIL.

The civil conflict resulted in the Arab league led by the Saudi Arabia and the organisation of Islamic cooperation to suspend Syria's membership. Russia and her allies, and China began to veto western drafted UN council resolution as early as 2011 and prevented additional sanctions, to be imposed on the Syrian government, already in the midst of chaos, civil war, estrangement and the threat of imminent collapse of Damascus and surrounding regions. These and other factors began to weigh in on the Syrian civil war. There were several allegations made of illegal weapons used in civil war, of cluster bombs, chemical weapons and heat weapons, which impacted on militia groups but equally civilians were caught in the crossfire. When it all was reported, Ban ki Moon, ordered a UN fact finding mission from the UNHRC and OPCW commission enquiry. Sarin the nerve agent was used in Khan al Assal, Saraqib, Ghouta, Jobar, Ashrafi Yat Sahnaya, in the year 2013. Three of the four places Sarin was confirmed. The commission noted the same hallmarks and reported to the United Nations. Despite the procedure, scattered ISIL and Syrian opposition and Turkish armed forces. The evidence gathering procedures began in earnest, through international agents and under UN security. In a report published in 2016, the UN and OPCW blamed the Syrian army of the Syrian government, for dropping chlorine bombs on the civilian populations.

No party claimed the attack; thus, the Syria government was named as the alternative suspect due to its possessing large arsenal of weapons. Towns of Talmenes and Sarnier, sulphur mustard gas were used by ISIS and in Mzerieb, in, the same year of 2015, in 2016, a similar incident occurred near Akrabat and breaking all records of 2013. In 2015, the UN security council adopted resolution 2235, to establish the joint investigation mechanism, to identify its preparators. A list too was compiled for these later, responsible in 2017, but was not made public. The report was passed onto the UN. The report for Khan Shaykhan attack was attributed to the Syrian government. The Syrian government made repeated claims, that the chemical plant east of Aleppo, had been captured, by rebel fighters from the Al-Nusra, front and they had stolen 200 tons of chlorine gas from the factory. The authenticity and discrepancies were explored and objections, continued between the Russians and the Americans. Sergey Lavrov the foreign Minister of Russia, then made a public declaration that Russia, had suggested to Syria, to relinquish its chemical weapons. The Syrian FM acted immediately and with deference to the proposal. The Syrian government signed the international agreements, for the destruction of all its chemical stockpile Russia, too carried, out its own investigation – the Khan al Asal investigation. The Russian ambassador Vitaly Chelien delivered a report with complete analysis of the samples. It was claimed that a rebel group with the free Syrian army Jaysh-al-Nasr brigade, had carried out the unfunded projectile chemical attack, the two sides did not agree. Russia FM Sergey Lavrov and Putin administration intervened, stating that Syria, had given the United States explanations and assurances that it was taking care of weapons. Members of Al-Nusra front had complied a toxic chemical weapon, into one or two places, to prevent rebel opposition forces, capturing them and using them. The Khan Shayk Hom chemical attack of 2018 also resulted in a swift response from the USA and France. In 2018, Un confirmed that yet again sarin, was used in the land that it came from Syrian government forces from the Syrian army stockpile. Peace efforts began by Sergey Lavrov and Putin, in Astana with UN arbiters presenting the Syrian government's point of view and based on the sovereign right of nations and Geneva, supported the SDF party, opposition to the government and was supported by the ideation of regime change at Geneva. Several international peace initiatives were fired off by the Russians. And some were undertaken by Saudi Arabia and USA in opposition to President Assad. The Syrian government claimed its right to sovereignty and legitimacy and refused to negotiate with those armed by the USA and her allies, against her integrity and sovereignty.

Russia under Sergey Lavrov FM in 2012, 2013, began the initiatives through Moscow, bringing to the table, the Syrian government and the opposition SDF. In 2014, US legal negotiations, were begun at the Geneva I conference, in Syria and took place, overseen by the UN envoy to Syria, and took place, overseen by the UN envoy to Syria, Lakhdar Brahimi. In 2016, UN mediated Geneva talks began, motivated by the international support group for the SDF in Vienna. Vienna conference was a stage for delegates from US, EU, Russia, China < Saudi Arabia, Egypt, Turkey Iran. Rebel leaders of SDF forces were not present in Geneva, Vienna or Moscow but in Nur Sultan in Kazakhstan in 2017. Astana was a preferred neutral venue, for peace negotiations between all groups. The negotiation with Arab league plans failed midway in 2011, 2012, and Russia's Putin, Sergey Lavrov began the initiatives, initially through informal talks' proposal, followed by the brokerage proposal conjoined with supporters for republic Syria and all were unsuccessful. The UNSG's too tried to wring in peace negotiations, with supporters for republic Syria and all were unsuccessful. The UNSG's too tried to wring in peace negotiations, with differing results. Geneva, I held under Kofi Annan too, did not yield a resolution, new fresh summits of nonaligned persons did not make headway, till the Eid-al-Adha, ceasefire attempt in September 2012. Under Ban Ki Moon, Geneva II, Astana Opposition conference, was supervised and the committee initiative started Zabadani Ceasefire agreement – through the Vienna process – the Riyadh conference, for Syrian opposition groups too was held separately. Now things began to happen and move in the right direction. The talks were suspended. In 2016, they began again, and Syria and Russia declared that discussing the legitimate president, of Syria in opposition to her, was a grave serious dangerous red line that could not be crossed. President

DIPLOMACY – ASTANA AND GENEVA TALKS CEASEFIRE DIPLOMACY – INITIATIVES IRAN.

Assad hoped that the talks in Astana and Geneva would result in good outcomes and stressed that change can only be brought about by an internal political process and not be interfering foreign nations, with vested interests in Syria's national resources and its vast reserves of oil and gas. In Astana, in 2017, Syrian government and Syrian rebels met in Astana and Kazakhstan with Russia, Iran, Turkey and UN officials present. The ceasefire agreement of December 2016 was discussed. The Astanan talks were a necessary complement to the Geneva talks and in 2017 May a further round of Astana talks were begun. The Syria peace process has been the most extensive ever and the initiatives and plans to resolve the Syrian civil war began at the onset. Russia instigated it first, followed by the Arab league and UN special envoy to Syria – The US allies too soon engaged the process, along with several European nations. The negotiations between Russia, Iran and Syrian Baathist governments and the Syria opposition, Kurdish forces did not partake in the Russian negotiations, framework and were backed by US and her allies. The Salafist, Islamic state of Iraq and Levant, were not part of the negotiations.

Quickly the Vienna process began, to make headway and Syrian women joined together to form a group, the Syrian women's advisory board, to get their voices and viewpoints heard. Finally, the cessation of hostilities began in early 2016 and a ceasefire deal was drafted. Led by John initiated complementary Astana talks and ceasefire options in December 2016. The Lausanne talks continued, and Astana conferences produced further ceasefires options in December 2016. The various nations, led by Russia emerged in several rounds of Astana talks in January, July, September, October, December 2017, and continued at Sochi talks in 2018. The Russians confirmed that the position of President Assad, had not changed with Abdel Basset Seda, present, whilst permanent members of the United Nations security council, held collateral talks with Martii Ahtisaari and Vitaly Churkin, and no conclusion was reached by either side. Turkey signed a memorandum the de-escalation zones, which came into effect, in May 2017. The reconstruction seemed, impossible but President Assad, stated he would rebuild a war-torn country. The reconstruction is estimated, in excess of US 900 billion dollars or even more. Russia have expressed concern, China and India have an interest in rebuilding Syria and later millions of refugees will have to be repatriated. The Syrian civil war has created a record refugee crisis and in two years. UN emergency aid handed over 6.5 billion dollars to Syrian opposition forces. An estimated 32,000 people had had been displaced, just by 2013. The United Nations office for the coordination, of humanitarian affairs, under Ban Ki Moon and in accordance with General Assembly, resolution 46/182 – assisted with sending billions of US dollars, between the years, 2011 – 2013. This was for the civilians and opposition forces, in the form of aid, medical supplies, emergency, basic health care, shelter and emergency relief supplies.

The world health organisation stepped up their efforts, as diseases novel and old emerged, due to the dead cadavers, lying on the streets with open wounds and escaping back to Tarsus, created a hostile contagion. Infectious diseases, affect the young mostly, children and the aged, and their conditions were fatal; leprosy began to surface, which had not been witnessed for decades if not centuries. Measles, typhoid, hepatitis, dysentery, bowel gut tract diseases, cancer of the brain, whooping cough and fatal skin conditions, consumed the very young and old alike. Leishmaniosis rose and mutant forms of contagious and crippling poliomyelitis, spread like wildfire, among the young and vulnerable. Many cadavers were recovered of babies and children, found under falling buildings and masonry. The displaced, rose to millions, almost half of the population was displaced. Some migrated to Lebanon, others to Jordan, Turkey, and Iraq, anywhere where they were safe, from falling bombs, sonic energy booms that rendered many blind and deaf, disease, dearth, destruction and mayhem. The towns of Deraa, Homs, Hama, cities of Turkey were besieged by refugees. Refugees from the 2013 Israel Gaza 100-day offensive too escaped either to Jordan or neighbouring nations. Libya, Syria, Iraq, Palestine, Gaza refugees mingled, in the safe haven nations. The spill over too, was like a human contagion, from all the conflict zones, in succession, one after another. ISIL was both in Syria and Iraq and took over large areas in Iraq, in fighting between rebel factions too, increased and this was seen in Lebanon, between supporters of Syria. In the years 2011-2019, heritage sites were looted, oil from oil fields was stolen and destruction of ancient relics was noted. IN Afrin, Arameans, relics were destroyed al I all, in over some 300 heritage sites were damaged and world heritage sites were totally destroyed. Antiquities were lost through shelling, sonic booms, looting and by Islamic groups infiltrating Syria from Egypt, Libya and Iraq and from northern Syria. UNESCO could do nothing, and UN had its hands tied. Syrian archaeological heritage some of the oldest was destroyed; items were stolen and traded in the black markets. Syria became endangered in more ways than one. Illegal digging was noted by Syrian archaeological heritage group and Palmyra and Krak des Chevaliers, were the most noted, as in extreme grave danger of extinction. The museums were looted and religious artefacts, in Raqqa disappeared overnight. The Islamic state of Iraq and Levant – ISIL in the periods 2011 to present, were destroyed by the joint actions of US and Syria and Russian air strikes. Ancient statutes of the temples of Baal Shamim, and Bel, the tower of Elahbel, the movement arch, the Palmyra castle, were all destroyed or extremely damaged in the Palmyra offensive as early as 2016.

Dier er Zour the Armenian Church, was decimated and works, were smuggled out of Syria, amidst the emerging chaos. United Nations estimated that the loss would be in excess of $ 400 billion. In Syria, we have seen the emergence of several cold war doctrines from the behaviour of Moscow, a reflection of the historic experience, and American behaviour as a reflection of the experience opposite to that of Russia. The cold war history of the two nations spans from 70 odd years since the world wars. The power vacuums were created in 1945, post the world wars through which Russia and America would expand, beginning with Europe. Russia in 1939-1940 conquered the Baltic states and east Poland and Stalin's post war intentions were revealed. Post war planning progressed slowly due to the divergence between American and Russian views of the world and the 1919-1945, there were extreme consequences, still erupting in Poland, and tragedies being suffered on an enormous scale in Poland. This was followed by the fall of Romania, Hungary, Bulgaria and Czechoslovakia. Conditions in Yugoslavia, Albania, Germany, Greece, Italy and France too were dire, post Hitler's campaigns in Europe and beyond the fall of Japan, resulted in the expansion of Russia and America's in the Far East. Amidst all this the United States struggled to find a workable foreign policy. The proclamation of the Truman doctrine came post 1947, after the Greek Turkish crisis of 1947 had settled. The Marshall plan was drafted drawn up delivered and Moscow reacted to it.

DIPLOMACY AND RECOVERY PROGRAMMES, LESSONS FROM EUROPEAN RECOVERY PROGRAMME.

Europe was shattered destroyed and, on her knees, and the European recovery programme, was begun by America and her allies in spite of Moscow's opposition.

The formulations of the cold war took on mythical issues and the Berlin Blockade resulted. Atomic power was to be feared after Hiroshima and Nagasaki and the western nation saw the implications and impact through its use on Japan and were reluctant to rearm.

The western military alliance resulted in NATO, and the far eastern policy, created horrendous disasters in the far east, till 1950 and beyond, but even right up to the present day. The Korean issue and war resulted in the success for the US and her allies, but angered China, provoking its rearmament in the United States and a powerful movement began to unite the European states.

Khrushchev tried again and later attempted to reshape the United Nations, the gamble of the USA and Russia in Latin America continued and in Cuba, Khrushchev's failure resulted in a new chapter in global politics. The US and Russia fought in proxy wars in Asian nations and far, east, with deadly consequences for the people of these nations and the very hot cold war spanning 40 years of proxy wars, began to slowly reverse and impact western nations, in a deleterious fashion, including Europe.

The Arabian expansionist movement with military European backing began with the Europeans who expanded into the Arabian Peninsula and the state of Israel was formed.

Thus, the United States and Russia became embroiled in the Arabian Peninsula, North Africa, Afghanistan and Asia in general and in specific. The balance of power established itself through diverse activities of the two nations, till the collapse of the USSR.

However, as the wars on Terrorism commenced in Afghanistan, North Africa and the Arabian Peninsula, the doctrine was in desuetude till the emergence of Russia and her allies into the system, in Suria, when it returned with a vengeance, and reactivated itself.

Both Russia and America had a sense of their mythology, and dignity and used every occasion to endow itself with nobility, in their causes for global wars.

Myths however are fictional Myths through sophistication can be transduced into concepts and through these principles are extracted, which can aid to interpret these principles are extracted, which can aid to interpret the existential world. This existential world constitutes all events, people and the world environment, through observations of the same; we can extrapolate, discern, and interpret facts to some degree.

Thus, man has to inhabit two worlds at once, the conceptual and the existential, and maintain a correspondence between both. Crisis emerges, when these two worlds' divers in an extreme manner and the world finds itself in very serious trouble at multiple levels.

Under the current circumstances of conflict between individuals and societies, between nations and within nations, and to the extent, that these conflicts become passionate, the conceptual formulations, of the universal rule of law, begins to degrade and get destroyed, and the paradigms of the two opposite world powers, America and Russia begin to move apart, diverse from the existential realities, each ostensibly represents.

At the base level, fear, hatred, self-justification, righteous rage, finds expression in deactivation of concepts and even falsification in advertent and deliberate. Whenever, an international conflict of the extent magnitude of the Middle east, Afghanistan, north south Korea, Latin America Africa break out, each power is impelled to construct.

What is its own advocate's account of the existential circumstances, by which power thus identifies itself with either representative or its opposite as evil?

This then is the crudest level which begins to activate and feed the world with deliberately fabricated propaganda. It takes myriad forms, some more corrupt, others less and people, are asked by its national leadership to sacrifice their luxuries and even their right to expression, happiness and comfort for the sake of some elusive victory, thus leaders begin to create myths and enter the domain of mythology, and thus ends and goals are justified and sacrifices are demanded. Struggles begin at the level of the man on the street, the capitalists against the republicans against the democrats and the proletarian against the capitalists and thus this becomes, the final destiny of all conflicts. The creation of myths enters a stratospheric contest between the aggressor nations and those that love and progress peace.

Thus, myths inspire the citizens to take up arms and fight, thus obviating any possibility of crowning success by a final conclusion of an elusive peace. This tragedy has been the same since the dawning of this century, with grave consequences for all of mankind. At the outsets there are specific objectives, or were of the USA and her allies however, specified as the rhetorical preference, the war on terrors.

Containing Russia for the USA is vital and in reverse the containment of the USA and her allies becomes paramount for the Asian nations and rejigging the fragile balance, of power. The objective to win is to prevent restoration, of any strength that is menacing and dangerous to the motives of a winning side. Post wars, the western strength was restored regardless of Russia's opposition and the same applies to the motives of the winning side. Post wars the western strength was restored regardless of Russia's opposition and the same applies now for the middle east nations and so checks and balances level in preventing expanding empires to move no further.

The Syrian civil war – Iran understood, first and foremost, what are the causes underlying the Syrian conflict or civil war through a narrow lens and scope, addressing domestic issues, the regional sectarian battles, the effects of the fallen states of regional sectarian battles, the effects of the fallen states of Libya and Iraq in the region, giving rise to the organised armies of the Islamic state of Iraq and Levant and ISIL in the region, and to examine key events between the years 2014-2017 focusing on major events, the peace negotiations, the activation of the balance of power with the entry of Russia and containment doctrines as applied to the State of Iraq, Syria and Levant (Islamic).

DIPLOMACY AND THE DOCTRINES OF BALANCE OF POWER.

The two main doctrines of balance of power and containment, which were key in the cold war, post the world wars, are seen afresh in Syria also impacting the region of the Middle East regions. The sudden intervention of Russia and her allies stand on regime change doctrine, impact the key events from 2014-2017 in the region and have resulted in implications for key- international relations diplomatic moves, other legal doctrines mainly with reference to Syria. The Syrian civil war has led to the singular reshaping of the Middle East its politics and introduced the shifting paradigms in flux since 2014 to present.

The focus on unique issues related to the civil war demonstrate, highlight and expand on the cascading events and consequences that have snowballed, bringing together east and west together on its larger issues and reinvolving the ideation and impact of the Sykes and Picot agreement that affected diversity, groups of peoples and the borders of Syria and its surrounding regions.

Latakia -In Latakia, the Syrian army had grown weaker and lost many positions, a development that resulted in Russia's deployment of troops. Earlier before Latakia, Russia had only sent military- advisors and technical support for the Syrian army.

The Syrian troops were only sent to Latakia and not Tartus which was Russia's official military base. Russia's presence, strengthening along the Syria coast as Assad's government's weakness, was greatest in this area and where Alawites do not constitute authority.

Latakia's demographics of its 40,000 populations were about 50% Alawite, 40% Sunni, 10% Christian orthodox, Alawites are still considered to be foreigners, by the urban dwellers. The French mandate, which began in 1920, the city had no Alawites and constituted only 100% Syrian

Arab Sunni population. The Adriatic shift occurred within the President Al Assad's policy of Alawitization which led to increased numbers of Alawites by 1980's.

Since Spring of 2012, the armed opposition controlled Jabal al Akrad, and the area along the Turkish borders up to the Armenian village of Kassab. In 2014 invasions occurred, in Kassab and destroyed the Russian radar station near Jabal Aqra. The Jihadist groups spread southward to the west of Idlib, Jisr-al-Shughou-r and Ariha – thus posing a real threat to the government's control in Latakia. The Syrian army, created the shield to the coast, to protect the coast, Given all the dynamics, the risk of a Sunni rising still exists although the Sunni suburb of Al Ramel al Filistini is controlled by the Syrian army since 2011.

Gaining access to the sea is strategic and symbolic for the rebels, the al-Qaeda affiliate, Jab hat al-Nusra, reached the Mediterranean in a matter of days. The Jaish al Fatah, also known as JN would have liked to control Latakia and Tartus.

Damascus and Homs were protected by Hezbollah and shite militias and Iran. Latakia, was strategic interest to Iran. Russia wanted to maintain a presence along the coast – more than in -Damascus or Golan Heights – Russia equally fortified the southern Turkish border, to prevent Sunni Syrian fighters, from gaining access to the sea.

The rebel's offensive thus near Idlib, meant that the Russians, Iranians, and Syrians had to act quickly, before they reached latakia. Rebel armies found strong support, from local Sunni residents, many due to their depraved conditions, longed and dreamed of revenge against the government. The fall of Jisr-al Shughour created fear, among the Alawite populations and families, who fled to Jabal al Ansariyya, in fear of their lives, from Latakia.

Russian escalation against the enemies of the state of Syria began in earnest. The Sunni population was growing, compared to the Alawite, and so the policy of the Assad government, was to push Sunnis out of the country, to rebalance demographics, in his favour. But Sunni refugees were pouring into Latakia, increasing security issues, in the area. The convert rebel elements increased and were known to be secretly embedded, with the refugees, waiting to attack Syria's forces.

Palmyra was lost to them. Assad stepped up measures to protect Alawite coastal areas, with the aid of Russian forces. In the meantime, Syria's Kurds were contemplating a role in Syria, with Assad and Russia,

The democrat's union party and the Syria franchise of the Turkish Kurdistan party PKK were eager, to connect to connect to Kobane and Afrin and open a Kurdish corridor in Aleppo. Assad had no option but to cooperate with them. US and Assad had no option but to cooperate with them. US and Assad had no option but to cooperate with them. US and allies had few options left, with Russia's intervention, but to do nothing, or play by the rules and secure the Syria peace process. Syrian Kurds were told they would not be allowed to gain more territory. The Sunni threat and rebellion remained from Kurdish Rojava.

Soon Aleppo, Daesh had launched an offensive north of Aleppo General Haedain's death, spurred Iran to intervene, more robustly in Aleppo. Russian aircraft increased their strikes and Russian ground troops entered Aleppo and Syria. By November 2015 great majority of Syrians began fleeing their homes because of Syrian attacks.

UNHCR released a figure of 120,000 people since the Russian intervention began, Syria's Assad was happy to see them leave, mainly Sunni Arabs, the attraction of Europe, due to a higher standard of living was a plus, healthcare, education, better integration, and a robust family reunion policy. The repression of the economic crisis increased the influx of Arab Sunnis from Syria, into Europe to make life bearable for them.

The geographical region of the Middle east is a desert and water or lack of it, is a determining factor of the start of the civil conflict.

Drought and failing water management and policies have shown that dry weather conditions have far outweighed any governmental policy in Syria and in the region as a whole. The external effects of the civil war have had an impact on refugees which were in Syria from the Gaza Palestine offensive of 2013, Libya offensive in 2011, and Iraq offensive from 2004-2008.

The Azaz corridor held a major strategic significance for Turkey, the corridor could not fall into the rebels, and Ankara was concerned. Russia waited to lock them out, at the Turkish cross borders, between Bab-al Hawa and Jisr-al-Sha-gur and placing Idlib in a single matrix, Russia held fort.

It was considered that a Kurdish offensive, would spin the risk of direct Turkish intervention, but equally it could isolate Islamic State, from the area. Again, the options for the west began to be restricted, but to close the states two-way route, through Turkey for good. The Kurds crossing the Euphrates was akin to the Roman emperor's crossing of the Rubicon, and history books were opened.

The first wave of Russian airstrikes, seemed to focus on rebel areas that threaten the Assad's government's Atlantic heartland, thus Moscow was more focused on seizing the mantle for Syria's war, rather than fighting terrorists, on the ground.

Russia streamed in with its air force, in cooperation with the Syrian army, led its first bombing strikes, in three of the country's provinces, Hama, Homs, and Latakia in the centre and northwest of the country.

DIPLOMACY AND THE ALEPPO HIGHWAY, SECURING TERRITORIES.

There was no Daesh Islamic state, ISIS, ISIL fighters in the area – the strategic goal, was to eliminate the rebel enclave and the rebels' occupying outskirts of Homs, were pushed out. The al-Qaeda affiliate, Jabhat - al Nusra, made local bridges, to pledge allegiance to them. Russia continued to strike in Latakia. The other targets were Mehardeh in Hama province, under threat from Jabhat-al-Nusra. Mehardeh is loyal to Assad but was surrounded by Sunni groups.

The Aleppo highway was critical strategy for Syria, and they could not get access to it.

Thus, a robust Russian intervention in Aleppo, and Catalina placed Moscow at the centre of the Middle East and Syrian chessboard. The wave of Russian airstrikes resulted in changing the game and securing the territory controlled by the Syrian armies.

Soon Russian strikes were coordinated with Syria, Hezbollah and Iran. The message was clear; the coalition against terrorism had been established with Syria, Iran Iraq and Hezbollah – Damascus swung into powerful action. Moscow was here to hit all groups it regarded as enemies of the State of Syria, including the Middle East, monarchies and even Turkey.

The Russians confirmed that the position of President Assad, had not changed, with Abdel Baset Seta, whilst permanent members of the United nations security council held collateral talks with Marti Antisaari, Vitaly Churkin and stepped up with a proposal of a three-point plan, which could enable Syria and her opposition to the negotiation table and even suggested that to bring peace, to the region. President Assad should step down. However, US, Britain, and France interjected, and rejected the proposal as they were convinced his fall was imminent and inevitable.

However, the stance changed, and Sergey Lavrov began to broken talks between Syria and the opposition, as both USA and Russian negotiations failed on the first round. Deputy FM of Russia, Bogdanov, suggested that Russia would engage with the conflict as well as humanitarian issues.

France and President Sarkozy, intervened to find a solution, after Russia and China had vetoed, a 2012 UN Security Council resolution. The 2012 talks yielded no result with the five permanent members of the UN security council, US Russia, China, France, UK, falling out after their FM Hillary Clinton suggested that Syria's Assad should be removed from office, but was countered by Sergey Lavrov. The talks were widely condemned by Arab Nations and by Ahar al-Shan. Tehran united 120 countries in 2012, to draw a new peace map for Syria, but again no consensus was reached.

The Joint special envoy for the United Nations, and Arab League made no true headway, neither did Geneva I 2012, Geneva II 2014, made no headway in this direction. In 2015, Astana conferences began and Staffan de Mistura was in charge. The ceasefire agreement resulted in a six-month truce between rebels, which held the town of Zabadin and Damascus and mediated in Russia's presence with Iran.

John Kerry FM of USA visited Russia, Moscow in late 2015 where he met with FM Sergey Lavrov as well as President Vladimir Putin and discussed UN resolution to be passed in New York, to endorse the agreement of the Syrian peace process.

In December the UN security council passed unanimously resolution 2254 (2015) which paved the way forward and set a timetable for a unity agreement in Syria in six months. Stefan presiding found, however that major Arab and global powers, remained undecided on this issue,

The Higher negotiation committee in Saudi Arabia drafted a common programme for Syria, supporting members were few and no position was conclusively taken. France, Saudi Arabia, Turkey, Qatar concluded the meeting. Geneva III tensions between Syrian government and opposition resulted in an unconstructive position on both sides, and the Syrian opposition wished to entrench preconditions.

The talks collapsed. Several Astana talks later, the head of the Syrian Arab republic delegation, called for immediate and unconditional withdrawal of foreign forces from Syrian territory and US forces. Exchanges of detainees, POWs missing persons were addressed as well as the implementation of de-escalation zones, in Idlib. In December 2017 Russia, made a public declaration that all terror groups had been arrested or quenched or cemented using the conversion doctrine and had surrendered and laid down arms.

Months later, President Trump declared that US troops were being withdrawn from Syria. The Golan Heights was a moot point and still remains so as Syria declared it is their sovereign territory and the natural oil and gas belongs to Syria although, the US and Israel made a joint declaratory saying it is Israeli property much the same way as Jerusalem, was declared capital of Israel, although it is true, to this day, is the holy place of three world religions Muslims, Christians, and Jews.

Dier al Zour, became the Middle Eastern Torgau, a German city where the US and Russian forces collaborated to defeat a mutual enemy. Once IS state of Iraq and the levant was defeated, (post wars in Iraq and Libya) the remnant military forces regrouped and the US and Russia cooperated against the Al Qaeda, remnants like Jabhat al Nusra in the region.

There were fresh concerns that the Islamic state of Iraq and Levant may resurface in the Golan heights. On the Syrian side, Assad had lost most of the Golan, the entire government's armoured divisions, had been withdrawn, to fight rebels in Damascus, Aleppo, and Hom's areas.

When President Trump had made a unilateral declaratory that Golan heights belonged to Israel and not Syria, Israel mixed airstrikes with humanitarian aid in the Golan heights.

The civil war added to these events and refugees and created complex anomalies with secondary and tertiary effects, in all of the Middle East, surrounding regions and posed a great threat to Syrian state stability, Russian allies, and Shiites, and housing crisis impacted all of these factors.

The ISIS (Islamic State of fallen Iraq and Libya) Levant armies coalition, Isil's ability to establish an independent state in Syria and Iraq was a direct threat to US global interests and security in the region, as the fall of Iraq and Libya created intense organisation by these groups as well as sectarian issues, and the attempts by ISIS and ISIL to unite disparate Arab groups.

These studies demonstrate the way by which Syria's civil war has impacted the Middle East, the international community and doctrines, instruments, paradigms, in key areas that were active at this time, in the middle east past 2001 or before. How these factors created the conflicts are paramount to understand, and equally to comprehend that conflicts of this nature are biological and dynamic things, and what emerges from the conflicts and analysis of these touches on geographical environmental, historical, current conflicts, key disturbances and events. Peace initiatives under international doctrines, and under international laws addressing humanitarian sectarian crisis, outside Iraq, Libya, levant, Syria even regions of Africa and other parts of the Middle east were ongoing.

Syria has seen a significant amount of activity from international actors, nations, domestic and global UN agencies, during the crisis both Inside Syria, Libya Levant, Iraq, Gaza, Palestine and other areas affected. The containment of Islamic state of Iraq and Levant are a serious challenge in the region.

DIPLOMACY IRAN AND WAR REFUGEES

There will have to be established a sustainable, water policy for refugees and in the long term the citizens, inhabitant of Syria. The conflicts show signs of slowing but after a major earthquake, like the Middle east conflicts the tectonic plates are still shifting. The spill over from four regions of conflicts continues to expand, Libya, Iraq, Israel, Gaza, Syria, with impenetrable curvatures that analysis cannot comprehend nor predict.

Syria is now a nightmare for the regions of the Middle East and North Africa, the entire Arabian Peninsula. The national systems of the state have been completely dismantled, every component of stability, has been impacted at the domestic, regional and global level, and sovereignty is in jeopardy with far reaching effects. The state instability and the fall out has broader implications for the region, the established paradigms in the economic sector, oil and gas, the peace process, Arab and Islamic politics. Arab Israeli relations, reforms, energy and economics, the-e Gulf energy policies, security and military proliferation issues, terrorism has increased as crime, which has increased exponentially in the region, and political violence copied from the IRA as paradigm has shaken up US policy like never before.

By now the battles raging were taking place in Idlib province and eastern Aleppo, both resulted in two million Syrians to depart for Turkey from northern western Syria.

Two safe zones were created outside the Kurdish and government held areas, one in Idlib province, the other in Aleppo province, both under Islamic state control. Those two areas were self-sufficient for food water, maintaining an open highway to Turkey was essential for medication and health services. Dier al Zour was the next battle fought in 2016, and US and Russia collaborated against the IS state. Given all the multiple factors operating in Dier al Zour, the fight against IS state was fundamental and mandatory.

A humanitarian disaster was inevitable stemming just from Syria, but from conflicts in Iraq, Libya, the neighbouring nations of Syria, but equally from the 100-day offensive conducted by Israel on the Gaza strip in 2013.

The disaster took on gargantuan proportions and refugees streamed towards the gates of Europe. The goal of a transition, no longer predicated Assad's departure. Syria was rightfully concerned about domestic terrorist threats a continued flow of refugees and hoping for the conflict to be contained in the balance of power was reinstated and using Putin's best lever for compelling Assad's enemies to cease all hostilities against a sovereign state. The West's choices were being diminished at an alarming state.

Two million refugees would end up in Turkey, Russia sought to east itself as the protector of the Syrian Kurds and presented a draft resolution to the UN security Council denouncing Turkish bombardment, of Turkish-villages in Syria continued. Its symbolic weight was clear, although the western powers rejected it outright. Ankara could be liable for breaking Turkish backed militias attacked the Kurdish allies in the democratic forces of Syria (DFS) i.e., Turkish Arab allies or if Turkey bombs Kurds another time. Turkey and Saudi Arabia were adamant for Bashar -al-Assad to step down. The Achilles heel of the ceasefire was that it excluded Jabhat al-Nusra and al-Qaeda affiliates that UN Washington and Moscow deem a terrorist organisation. Assad's call for election was consistent with the message with the constitution. Assad's call for election was consistent with the constitution, after five years of war with the Islamic state of Iraq and Levant, in both Iraq and Syria against Al Nusra and Al Qaeda terrorist organisations.

The ongoing military and political strategy of Russia was to secure Assad's rule. In 2016 amid a ceasefire in Syria, Assad declared Parliamentary elections would be held on April 13th.

The ceasefire, gave Russia a break after a major offensive, launched a few weeks in which Syria and its allies, won territory-al gains under the backing of formidable Russian air power. Russia waited, Ankara, Turkey to withdraw its support from the opposition forces and to close its borders. It reiterated that if Turkey did not, there would be consequences –

thus using both carrots and sticks. Israel along with US and allies, watched the Golan heights, it was monitored and managed, to prevent takeover by Islamic state of Iraq and Levant, who claimed to be enshrined as the true defenders of Islam.

The Syrian civil war to its historical, religious significance, since roman times, has garnered attention like no other place in contemporary history and politics has failed to follow the pattern of other Middle Eastern nations with which the US went to war against under the terrorism paradigm, i.e.., Iraq, Libya, Gaza Palestine, and Yemen. It has failed to follow the pattern too of the Middle eastern states, where revolt movements have sprung up i.e. if not global nations engagement has followed a decidedly different trajectory. The nature of the Arab revolt or Arab spring in Syria is complex and is the only place where the civil war impacted in manner never seen in living history. The air strikes too have created regions to become unstable, depopulated, as the joint forces try to contain ISIS, ISIL from gaining a stronghold in key regions, around Damascus. What began as a small revolt activated nations, and superpowers on two sides of each other Russia and USA and equally Saudi Arabia and Iran. The results could have been more devastating but for the attention of the international community, and a devastating humanitarian crisis was effectively contained by superior leadership and agencies. However, the conflict has had significant effects on international law, principles, paradigms and instrument, leading to external and internal consequences. The refugee's exodus was curbed, enabled to safe zones, and the rise of ISIS and ISIL original state members and non-state actors brought various groups to come to a head in the region. The expanding effects of Syria resulted in reversing the regime change policy and to promote sovereignty by the United States and Russia, and this was to reshape the Arab world in its entirely.

DIPLOMACY STABILITY AND FRAGILITY INDEX.

Civil war has jeopardised Syria's stability resulting in a high-ranking state fragility index. The institute of Peace considers Syria as the 15th most fragile nation and on high alert for state failure. Fragility skyrockets if there is extreme violence, in and around a state in multiple forms.

Since 2020, Syria became a gradually more and more fragile till it was in the top percentile of unstable states.

Researching ongoing events presents numerous challenges. Only reliable data, facts, have to be studies in an e-diplomacy channel, engaging with those involved, both behind the scenes, as decision makers or on the ground in Syria as security forces or air bases involved with the same procedures and process.

Very few peers reviewed scholastic work is around and multiple analytical and research methods have to be applied, with constantly evolving date, case studies, news reports and a combination of other forums and methods, hosting debates conferences, listening to invited speakers from various nations. The best evidence has to be selected to gain understanding of the many complicated issues related to the Syrian civil war.

Water needs, not met for farming lands, drove farmers to urban centres to find work, thus creating mass populations to move out of farming, regions cities. The unemployed citizens joined the revolt against the governments bad or inadequate policies and provisions.

Some of these issues could have been avoided, if the government had established, complemented and enforced agricultural trade, policies and proper regulations, fit for purpose.

The devastating effects of the civil war are to the Syrian people, themselves. The United nation's estimated that there were four million refugees created by the war. Figures vary from different census and from institution to institution.

The violence impacted, the civilians as rebel fighters, Islamic radical groups, foreign armies, Islamic state of Iraq and levant, all surrounded them creating a massive chaos and produced the worst human crisis of this generation.

Turkey Lebanon, Jordan all hosted refugees with a huge strain on their resources. Studies using various statistical tools and analysis by various scientists, showed a positive correlation between the refugees and overall state stability.

The formation of the fallen states of Iraq and Libya produced the Islamic state of Iraq, Syrian and Levant, henceforth addressed as ISIL and ISIL, hoped to overturn the borders established by the Sykes Picot agreement at the end of the colonial rule in the Middle East. Redrawing state borders would bring in Shia, Sunni, Kurds all under one roof and thus ISIS would having redefined Syria's borders and established a unitary system called Islamic state.

There are many Arab and Islamic issues, which have resurfaced post the Obama administration, i.e., Iran and the Khamenei's position, show how the USA, now wishes, to return to the re-negotiating table, under the Trump administration rather than going for all-out war with Iran, post Syria. Iran has always been a supporter of the government of Syria and President Assad, since the beginning of the civil war and remains in the Russian balance of power axis, and thus puts it's in a vulnerable position, with opposing USA views on Syria and regime change.

The chances of extracting substantial concessions from Ira, America knows are not great, and Secretary of State Mike Pompeo, warned Iran (Post the Obama administration set up of the Iran deal), that the Trump administration would continue to ratchet up, the pressure on Iran, and despite the dogged campaign, to further tighten sanctions, the supreme leader of Iran has pushed the Iranian nation to resist US policies towards it and the renewed sanctions being imposed on its nation and populations.

Iran's resistance policy, hinges on innovatively circumventing draconian economic restrictions, which have beleaguered a rich nation over several decades, and through several USA administrations.

Iran continues to be part of the Russian side of the balance of power doctrine and supports the idea of national sovereignty, and freedom from interests by foreign powers. Thus, the defiant stance continues as adversaries rather than unequal nations. Iran in spite of the changed Iran policy, remains diametrically opposed to much of the USA's middle eastern policy, and the most recent evidence of its balance of power status, was positively seen in the decision to appoint general Hossein Salami, as commander in chief of the National defence forces, the Islamic revolutionary guard corps, almost as soon as the Trump administration designated Iran's defence forces the IRGC, as a foreign terrorist organisation, much to the upset felt by Russia and her allies, in the balance of power axis. Iran sees it as trampling of its national rights, sovereignty, and identity, right to seek self-determination, arrested development and progress.

Naturally these moves would have been seen as defiant, before the advent of Russia in the Middle East politics, and Americans under President Trump have had to reevaluate their policy, and address circumstances, under which the Iranian government, would be willing to return to the negotiating table and discuss afresh, the nuclear programme, the missile programme and its policy towards Syria and the region.

Other policy issues have arisen, since Syrian conflicts began such as making sense of Iraq's arrests of the PMF (the popular mobility forces), and the equally difficult issues of Israel's armistice, growing tensions between Palestine and Israel, Hamas and Abbas, the leader of the Palestinians in the state.

The Palestinians continue, to reject President Trump's peace plan. The Palestinian-Israel relations are the reason for the focus and angst among other Arab nations, in the region, again on the principle of national sovereignty and integrity.

The soured relations, animosity and resentment continues, unabated and the Arab Israel in a wider sense have recently spelt out that Jared Kushner's peace plan would be a disaster and that renewed interventions by President Trump with the current Israel – Palestine position, would turn the Middle east into a danger zone.

There are growing concerns, of Arab nations, on democracy and reform, talks about the Iraq-Turkey oil pipelines, with arbitration advisers wishing to renew the policy in the areas of energy and economics in the region of the Arabian Peninsula, North Africa and Yemen.

A disorganised army of fallen states such as ISIS and ISIL did not have the methods needed to be successful in uniting diverse peoples that makeup the vast Arabic world. The tactics used by ISIS and ISIL would encourage more divisions and push Kurds towards the Anglo-American supporters to establish an independent state for them.

Cumulatively the complexity of the many interwoven factors, multipliers have continued to mutate expand and distort the Syrian civil war. The core issues when addressed must aim to restore stability in Syria and the Arab world, restore peace in the region, alleviating natural and regional problems, resolving issues along sectarian lines.

Arabia is a desert island, and many factors precipitate around this one point. Arab socialism, political ideology, economic distribution dynastic rule, corruption from within and external factors all contribute to the civil war. Heart, dearth of water, impacts on the man of Syria and the nations, this is seen to occur globally, the role water plays in the development and economics of Syria is not the only dry nation in the world in terms of natural water resources.

Syria needs to carefully calculate the water per capital and for agriculture. The Syrian government, policy was to relocate water towards agricultural and commercial endeavours leaving minimal cubic metres per capital for consumptions, thus leaving people with no shortage of water. Water or dearth of it, can have devastating effects on the lives of people, crop failure, breakdown of economics, and thus social structures in Syria.

The agricultural decay soon led to structural decay and resulted in the eventual migrations to city centres and thus exacerbates unemployment, economic decline, and eventually eruption of social unrest. Many scholars have shown the connection between economic crisis civil conflict, unrest and violence against political leaders. Political grievances are highlighted.

Water management thus was one of the key policies that impacted on the unrest and rise of Arab spring.

Noted scholars of the Arab Asiatic worlds have provided key insights to governance of power structures in a place of water shortages. The dynastic monarchical, authoritarian rule, dependence on agriculture, oil reserves, governance and religion, state ownership of land and energy resources are key means of production. Agricultural societies after the landowner holds absolute power and corruption can seep in, thus they hold sway over all matters.

In a state where agriculture is the main profession, then absolute power leads to control of administration managerial, energy and oil, crops judiciary, military and financial control and make laws as whey they- see fit, propaganda, and coercion can be used to gain control.

In a state where agriculture is the main profession, then absolute power leads to control of administrative managerial, energy and oil, crops judiciary, military and financial control and make laws as when they see fit, propaganda and coercion can be used to gain control.

Thus, the rule of governance becomes authoritarian very quickly. In the Arab world, Shia law determines the legitimacy of a ruler, and government and religious power go hand in hand.

Thus, as a rule of the religious establishment, the ruler establishes his legitimacy as a despot, monarch or authoritarian ruler.

Dynastic and Monarchical republics demonstrate that autocracies often have the dynastic ruler with its dominant regimes of religious leaders, nobles, political elites on one side and his democracy or republic as a secondary from governance.

United Kingdom is a classic example and is a functional monarchical democracy with the sovereign as the head of state.

In Syria, a republic has a president, as the head albeit through elections, he hails from a dynasty and hence is not seen as one of the people, with his father a President before him. This is not strictly a power monopoly but prima facie, it appears to be so. However as Monarchies died out in the western hemisphere, and most eastern nations too, some remained and retained it such as the United Kingdom, some minor scattered principalities of Europe, France abandoned it, India too, which has seen dynasties of kingdoms one after another for millennia, as did some Arab nations, but equally others retained it such- as Saudi Arabia which is represented by the Royal house of Saud, just as the House of Windsor, represents the United Kingdom or principality.

The mind of democracies and monarchies are different as well as republics and understanding the mentality of the dynastic rule and its governance is /0/ useless in interpretation the events of the Arab spring and new Arabic theories, state that there are constant movements to overthrow authoritarian regimes, in favour of a more legitimate popular and people's representative governments.

A republic under a state of emergency, like a civil war, can quickly transform to authoritarian and emergency powers activated giving the ruler the power to confiscate, property, land resources, eliminating all opposition and consolidating life in all its forms, and the rule to protect the sovereignty of the principal of the state.

Without a civil war too certain Arab states have been accused of holding unchecked power over state functions and becoming despotic, their power is rationalised by the need to secure large oil reserves or agricultural irrigation.

Economic shocks too can accelerate civil conflict, negative growth shocks result in a drop in economic growth, the young joined armed fighters, and are linked to rising of potential grievances and ethnic groups divide ethnicity, insurgency and civil war.

These studies were considered in Africa and do not translate to Arabian countries to different ideologies thinking, history, oil culture and environmental factors.

Syria gained independence in 1946 and experienced more than three decades of turbulent power transitions. However, things began to settle in 1963, the Baath party came to power and was founded as a national party promoting Arab interests, and calling for the union of the Arab states, much like the European union today.

The party was led by intellectual leaders and officers from all background and from all regions. They promoted development, aiding farming, irrigations, rural lands, and they learnt from the Russians and their policies that modernised oil, energy projects, including the Euphrates region. Thus, the infrastructure investments would in the long-term benefit agriculture.

Hafez Al Assad established state departments, revolutionised governance and established ties between state and agricultural, oil economies. He was depicted as the father of the nation of Syria.

He established the Syrian parliament and a permanent Syrian republic constitution, thus consolidating presidential power, over all of Syria's institutions, including local governments and military. These actions thus established governments and military. These actions thus established governments and military. These actions thus established the founding ideals and transitioned Syria into a republican democracy. Syrian republic saw the countryside as rich sources of potential wealth, but equally was aware that Syria's economic resources and capital was the envy of the rival groups, factions within Syria and the wider Arabian world.

Thus, control of agricultural and energy forms of Syria were the key political strategy adopted by President Hafez-al Assad's government to keep the republic flowing smoothly through all of its regions.

Hafez Assad died in 2000, transferring his role to his son, Bashar-al-Assad as President of Syria, Bashar was looked upon favourably, he was young dynamic and his key policy objectives were to change both oil explorations in its many fields, as well as to enhance agriculture.

Self-sufficiency led to greater and bolder decisions to expand irrigation in its rural areas. It was this same need that was deterred in 1973 by the oil price shock, and when the price of food became a bargaining tactic, to counter the price of oil.

Food was essential to Syria, so it placed it as a priority. Through the passing of legislation, it enabled the state to order which crops to grow, where and when, and setting the price for them. By setting prices, such that it incentivised farmers to grow strategic crops. Later policy decisions helped to facilitate infrastructure.

IRAN DIPLOMACY AND POLICY OF SAFE ZONES.

Later policies took steps to aid regulation of oil and farming sectors. One impacted on the other, and corporations boomed. Provisions, were made for tax free low interest loans, subsidizing transport to markets, these policy decisions, increased farming and industrial products, and however there were some that were a threat to ground water extraction, reserves, and that it deplete the already low water table to extremely low levels, all in all by the 1950's. Syria was rising and the population was booming increasing exponentially from 3.3 million people to 20 million in 2014 and to 50 million by 2050. However, this trend erupted suddenly by wars in the region.

The unrest in the region, resulted in mismanagement of resources corruption and these drove the system in a war-torn region at the brink of collapse. The tribes began to disintegrate, unemployment increased and there was no more legitimate ruling possible under the principles of Sharia or Islamic laws.

The conditions became desperate, and unemployment became rampant, and revolution incited and ignited further the civil war, global warming, and climate change compounded by conflict, in the region, resulted, in acute water shortage, and Syria became a victim to both climate change, unfortunate weather patterns, suddenly and violently.

Syria's five zones became drier and drier affecting the farmers and Bedouin tribes. This resulted in extreme socioeconomic consequences.

Drought increased with the civil war and hit the entire region, Iraq, Syria, Israel, Jordan, Lebanon and Palestine; however, it led to severe malnutrition and mass migrations. Drought magnified the effects of poverty and farmers in the steppe land saw decreased rainfall and temperature increases. The phenomenon could not be explained by overgrazing or any other reason. Ecologist stated that the flora fauna in the region adapted to changes and could normally adapt to altered weather patterns and for long period of droughts, but this time, it did not. In Al Talila, nature reserve, desertification was seen like never before. The vegetation did not recover, and green pastures, were gone with increasing desertification.

The ecosystem became imbalanced and the steppe land once fruitful became barren.

According to the United Nations, when the drought broke out, 800,000 farmers overnight lost their livelihoods. The governments tried to take steps to reduce it, the oil production fell sharply, price of oil rocketed, increasing the cost per barrel, lands could not be irrigated, crops failed, transport to market ceased.

The demands for increased and expansion of refugees, contributed to further drastic changes. Immigration failed due to lack of water, food became scarce, and subsidies mounted increasing pressures on the people and systems.

The United Nations food and agricultural organisation estimated that the country's production of wheat dropped dramatically to a quarter of its annual average creating a severe food crisis. The fiscal policies prior to the civil war, did not work anymore. The US department of agriculture had once reported that Syria had during the high price of wheat in the international market, sold its excess reserves of 2.5 million metric tons of wheat prior to the civil war beginning. But post the civil war, the drought reduced production, and Syria was forced to import wheat, a sad state of affairs.

DIPLOMACY AND HUMANITARIAN CRISIS IRAN AND RUSSIA

Syria scientists and economists write that the populations of Tigris and Euphrates, rivers began leaving in the last decade, creating a refugee crisis for Syria. The cities were overcome by their arrival.

Some of these refugees became disenchanted and hence politicised. In Ancient Mesopotamia, the role of governments was to manage policies for farmlands, water and irrigation systems. With the discovery of oil, the policies shifted. The Syrian government found conditions, worsening, with unemployment and water shortages.

The twenty or so government agencies became understaffed resulting in the exploitation of Syria's natural resources and ancient artefacts. The regulations in the face of wars were unsustainable.

It was impossible to recruit educated staff and poor wages resulted in corruption. Sophisticated, policies were drafted but never implemented. Delaying drought policies resulted in a growing humanitarian crisis as early as 2006, prior to the drought of 2010. Implementing sustainable policies was vital, but the inability of the government resulting in a worse humanitarian crisis.

Providing aid was inadequate, managing water conservation sites, impossible, the result worsening situation in and around Syria. Strategically Syria failed statistically in conservation plans for vulnerable regions.

The water agencies were depleted of resources, lacked good governance, procedures and plans to move things forward quickly.

The government, however, went ahead, invested in rebuilding, infrastructure, established, and subsidies, other relief measures, but which began to further empty the state's coffers. Syria drew up plans to establish and adhere to a realistic policy, a plan that would alleviate the situation in Syria.

Syria recommended transparency, to evaluate, the accuracy of incoming data, and thus allow its experts to formulate a clear regulatory- framework, to enact, enforce water and energy-related guidelines. Policies pertaining to farming, drilling, irrigation, were improved and modernised, to improve food crop growth, efficiencies. In irrigation, and drilling systems. Consolidating the government bodies key, and people with requisite skills were brought in to wring in the changes, and provide scrutiny to reduce corruption, bad practices, and nepotism, operating in the ranks.

Thus, environmental factors, altered weather patterns, played a significant role in Syria's civil war. The Syrian government had no time to enforce environmental policies or drought policies, and the rising populations, became a greater internal destabilising factor, than any other.

These areas of emergency improvements thus became an impossible task in the midst of chaos and a growing civil war.

Thus, an alternative system of power, rose through the civil war and threatened the government and its task to provide clear governance frameworks, to stabilise Syrian people and society.

The Iraq and Libya crisis had already impacted Lebanon, Israel, Palestine, Jordan and Syria.

Now the other states surrounding Syria faced increasingly precarious stability, security, threats, sectarian conflicts, discord among tribes, began to characterise Syria, by sudden onset of Arab spring, uprisings, fighters, networks began to float in Syria foreigners, transnational zealots and suddenly there were violent deaths in Syria, most civilian casualties more than third of the population, fled in a mass exodus.

Syria's neighbours were gutted with refugees. Lebanon was the first to bear the brunt.

This was a new type of conflict, a new war, and could be conceptualised into the analytical paradigms of modern contemporary wars and conflicts. Network of states can be fed into and along with non-state actors, and the war involves different methods of findings, and those involved gain in political and economic ways from violence itself rather than an end stage of winning or losing.

Modern warfare thus can be seen as a movement which imposes ethnic religious and identity divides simply for the purpose of claiming power. This new model can be seen by understanding Syrian war in all of its ramifications, all the hostile actions, within the area, and by external forces and how the region at large is impacted on a social, economic, political and human level.

If legitimate governments fail to take the right actions at the right time, to create favourable environments for its inhabitants, keeping out unwanted peoples, attacks on civilian institutions, places, economic destruction, and violence, the result would be that entire populations will be driven out of the state.

Population displacement is a war technique to conduct a war against a nation, and Syria is the key model of its application. A mass exodus of refugees, itself, becomes a trigger for more violent conflict and a larger regional dispute.

Lebanon with a massive influx of refugees, created a national crisis, and was labelled so by the United Nations. Tensions increased in Iraq, in Gaza and Syria, and they all had a tremendous impact on each other and the human condition.

A refugee is already a person grounded in fear, of persecution, on the basis of race, ethnicity, nationality, memberships of groups, political opinion, and is alone in another country, from its own nationality, and is thus unable to avail the protections of that country, and cannot return to its own for fear of being killed, or persecuted.

Syrians their thousands arrived in Jordan, Turkey, Lebanon, and into other neighbouring nations.

DIPLOMACY CRISIS MANAGEMENT IRAN AND LEBANON

Before the crisis, Lebanon was on the not the most stable, but all areas and countries around Syria were affected state fragility, can be measured by many factors, such as no authority to make decisions, loss of territory, inadequate, public services, no diplomatic ability, to interact with other nations Lebanon saw a cruel war lasting a long time, and it is still trying to regain its footing. Its displaced population, lies all over the Middle east, and influx into Lebanon, has resulted in friction between the refugees and native Lebanon populations can lead to strength and success, in the long term but if sudden and overwhelming, it can lead to state rupture, fracture and increased fragility, and even future death and failure.

Sending and receiving states need to understand the concepts of international relations. Migration often links up with political decisions, making in an urgent sense, as the global perception in times of conflict is that migrants will be unstable, and hence threatening, within the new set up and environments. Refugee presence thus can have a direct bearing on foreign policy decisions.

Asylum issues can often cause strife, there are humanitarian problems, state stability and security problems for the host country.

Refugees have been associated with creating chaos in host nations due to their unstable mentality, having left conflict zones. The spillover effect can be of enormous magnitude.

The influx of secondary and tertiary freedom fighters is real, and regional conflict can break out, and is evidenced as read due to the macro effects of the refugee movement. There is always the added risk of terror organisations to infiltrate weakened states.

There are additional unintended consequences of internal crisis, the number of refugees has significantly increased over time. The Islamic state of Iraq and al-Sham increased over time. The Islamic state of Iraq and al-sham also truncated as ISIS, IS or ISIL, rose after Iraq and Libya conflicts. Members called all to follow the leadership of Abu-Bakr -Al-Baghdadi, who they claimed was a direct descendant of Prophet Muhammad.

This was a threat to Syria as they wished to establish Islamic governance and redraw state lines. The end of the Sykes-Picot was in sight. Sykes-Picot was created in 1916, when a deal as struck between France and the United Kingdom, when certain areas of control of the Ottoman Empire, were made, so it would not fall into the hands of the triple entente.

The Treaty terms divide Middle East between areas of Arab French and British control. Each of them, had to define the state boundaries within the area of control and it proved to be a success as it provided stability to a volatile region and chaotic region.

What was not considered were the long-term effects of segregating inhabitants of the region and ethnic sects? No one foresaw that sects would eventually play a significant role in Middle east politics. Two major Middle east states are in direct competition for rule in the area, Iran a Shia state and Saudi Arabia which is a Sunni state. The Iraq state played a significant role in the creation of ISIS, primarily the de-Baathification policy followed 9/11 and post Saddam Hussein. ISIS thus began its operating in Iraq then Syria with a view to reclaiming both regions of Iraq and Syria.

Thus, ISIS began to go along with the Syrian rebel fighters to control a large portion of Syria. Added to this complexity Syria Kurds joined forces with Kurds of Iraq and began to clamour with western powers to establish an independent state.

Ethnic strife, passions, divisions are Arabia's nature and foundation. Historical events antecedents must be understood and are critical to evaluate Arab ideology and historical antecedents.

Arab rule is based on autocracy and its foundation is monarchs as old as time itself and how grievance links with religion in the Arab world,

world politics, uses the Shia and Sunni historical difference, and influences sectarian conflict in the Middle east. These ancient historical findings provide context and frameworks to understand sectarian crisis and from which principles of life as it works in the Arabia's can be drawn.

Isis is fundamentally the rise of nationalism in Arabia. Once the Sykes Picot agreement was established, Arab nationalism rose in the province in the region. This ideology became the most basic way of thinking in the Arabia and the Arabs see their world as one stretching from Saudi Arabia and Persia to cover all the Gulf states.

The Levant which comprises Islamic world in North Africa too is an adjunct of mainland Arabia. They are bound to Arabia through religion primarily and all the consequences that stem from it secondarily.

The Arabs see the Sykes Picot agreement as a division instrument and which was used to share the spoils of war among France, and UK and thus were vesting their best interests in oil rich fertile lands, whilst ignoring the true interests of the Arab peoples.

The era post Gamel Abdel Nasser, the leader of unification of Arab states, and his loss of authority post the six-day war resulted in a different form of Arab nationalism movement.

Thus, the unification of Arabia failed, and gave way to a new system of independent states each requiring its individual national sovereignty, rather than to perform a union of Arab nations, similar to the European union, based on shared religion, history, values belief systems, and ideologies. Arab fundamentalism was in the end for Arabia as a whole a disastrous ideology, and post Nasser, Arab nations, aligned and even joined forces with the United states, against other Arab nations to seek liberation during interregional wars, a Kuwait war in 1911, the gulf war, which cemented strong partnerships with the west and oil exports increased from Arabia or middle east into the international oil market.

Thinking the unthinkable a sovereign Arabia melted into the archives of time, as fundamentalist Arab awakening, grew and with it the Arabia national movements. Arabia as a whole thus vacillated from disaster to triumph to fresh disasters.

In North Africa, changes impacted the Arab lands too; the ousting and toppling of President Ben Ali of Tunisia and Mubarak of Egypt resulted in a violent resurgence of Islamic versus Arabic identity, to Libya, Morocco, impacting Bahrain, Syria and Jordan.

DIPLOMACY AND AFRICAN REVOLTS SPILL INTO ARABIA

Thus, competition between North African states and revolts spilled into Arab too and they were strongly linked. The sense of Islamic ideologies and protests spread all over the North African states called the Arab spring movement, into the adjacent Arabian states. It spread as an interdependent transcontinental transnational movement into quintessential Arab worlds. It was a new political result influenced by structures and peoples pushing politics into a new political direction. This however contrary to media portrayal was far from a unifying theme and was distinct from Arabian which called for a union of Arab states whilst each one maintaining its sovereignty.

The unilateral consequences of the Shia movement ignited conflicts between North African Islamic Pan Arabian groups who were Sunni and Iran led forces which were Shia. Arabia was reproduced a new every single day and power legitimacy were and peace making between life at Arabian and pan Arabian coalitions led to increased ethnic conflicts and imparted international politics in the middle east.

The overflow of Saddam Hussein's Sunni government and transfer of power to Shia fostered a joking relationship between Iran and Shia politics began to become pre-eminent. This ascension united the Saudi Arabian nation and Sunnis especially.

The Arab peace or transformation can only take place if and when there is distribution of resources wealth, opportunities in an equitable manner. Only through introducing policies via grievance structures, that are in place a much more utilitarian and just system, thereby-introducing reforms which would bring in the needs of the people, the doctrine of Arabia forms of proportional representation of tribes, Alawite, Shia, Sunni, Kurds and other minorities into the system, thereby reducing oppression caused by flawed policies or governance procedures in substance and form.

The region must therefore align itself to republican democratic and natural justice systems within its monarchical or even dictatorial style politics.

This can be obtained similar to monarchical democracies or dual run systems in the United Kingdom and other. European models, which have either retained their monarchies for historical and functional means or have abolished them replacing them replacing the Monarch with a republican president, and hence a president. The Arabian region thus must undergo an enlightened transformation.

Western nations must comprehend that autocratic rule stems from its historical power structures, its root, foundations and ancient governance structures, especially prior to the discovery of law, the archetypal systems of monarchical autocratic or dogmatic systems stem from dependence on agriculture in desert lands and link this to religion, heavy reliance on providence and thus governance. In Syria state ownership of agricultural lands is vital for the nation's survival.

Dominance in governance is necessary as dynasties for legitimacy of rule and to bring in together, religious, political, intellectuals and traditionally An Arabia this power monopoly has always been understood as both historical and contemporary.

What the west has labelled as despotism and has used this as a lens to interpret all events is actually the norm of Arabic jurisprudence, governance, political and social structures since ancient times.

The ideation of Arab spring new Arabian theories created by intellectuals in the USA and UK primarily misunderstood the quintessential Arabian paradigm and this misinterpreted the flow of concepts from this region, and thus advocate overthrow of autocratic dominant power structures or using a derogatory term, overthrow despots, and authoritarian regimes, in favour of milder no dynastic people chosen representatives who in their eyes will stay away unrest, and bring about cohesion in Syria and wider Arabian nations.

However dynastic rules and their governance can hold great unchecked power over the population, but also over all state functions, ranging from the domestic police, military, executive, judiciary, legislative and religious institutions and the lands.

Despotism is the converse of democracy, or even dynasties, where a dictatorial despotic government or ruler, regime or structures can abuse power, to confiscate land property, wealth, resources and deter opposition in a brutal manner, extinguish all competition, and thus link everything in a draconian fashion, consolidate wealth, power, financial property and adhere it to promote themselves, their rule with total disregard for life, humanity, ethics, natural justice in all its forms.

The kind of abusive power cannot and should never be rationalised justified and normalised by legitimate nations, and the united or international community or civilised unions of nations in the world.

Dominant rulers however seek benevolence of the lands, people and sovereignty although it is based on the notion of good news, ethics and justice albeit not a republican capitalist nor a totally democratic structure as acknowledged through ancient Greece and roman traditions.

As in all nations, the degree of corruption, correlation with corrupt officials and or policies within systems who seek not benevolence but are driven by gains and agendas, thus leading to a corrupt governance, gross mismanagement, of nations resources and during a nation or nations through self-interest rather than nationhood almost posing it to deterioration or even the brink of collapse and degradation.

The populace begins to revolt, lose faith in the ruling elite or powers do not trust or consider them as honest, filled with integrity or even legitimate thus opening up doors for unrest, insurance of lawlessness and even civil revolution.

What the Sykes Picot agreement means for Syria is that foreign nations have constantly wielded subtle influence on the nation in myriad forms which could be tantamount to gross interference in its internal affairs.

Leaders in Syria have had problems, to let go of this notion over time and feel their legitimacy and the sovereignty integrity of their nation, has been constantly at stake since then and hence the legitimacy of their governments its people, citizens, ethnic groups, religious sects temperament and temper has always been vulgarised and misrepresented to the world therefore undermining their legitimacy and thereby degrading the valid and unable opportunities of the nation, to grow, develop and advance using skills and natural resources.

DIPLOMACY AND DEALING WITH COMMON ARABIAN ISSUES IRAN, LEBANON AND SYRIA

Under these circumstances of interference, a polity of shock and awe, degrade and destroy escalating sanctions through time and place have resulted in underdeveloped and sophisticated equitable systems as the nation's constantly find themselves under threat of being taken over, by foreign powers and which as a result, causes divisions, preferences giving rise to tax.

Result in unequitable distribution of resources among nations, groups, tribes, minorities, citizens and giving rise to preferences of certain groups, thereby leading to a much more expansive sectarian conflict, which spreading through the Arabian regions via Syria.

This resurgence of fundamentalism, extreme nationalism, witnessed in ethnic groups, and a return to Sharia law, is evidence of the breakdown in strategic structures of legitimate departments and systems. Internally longstanding problems, in society, grievances towards authority and legitimacy of Arab nations, as their Arabic societal foundations are rocked due to internal differentiation and conflicts.

The new Islamic fundamentalist view is opposed to the traditional Arab unitary view, which accords to the stratagem a region consensus, rather than a single state and a central command authority which will lend itself, better to dealing with common Arab issues.

The recent conflicts in the Arab region undermine this approach, and due to unrest, shifts, desertification. The Arab world and in the main USA and UK have resulted in a deterioration and even waning of this idea in the Arab worlds.

Arab governance in Syria and other Arab nations do not seem to be interested anymore in pan Arab world it gives the opportunity.

The analysis of Syria and surrounding Arab nations or regions has shown of how pan Arabia will not materialise in the near future, due to the agendas of transnational militia groups that infiltrate and undermine them in contemporary times.

The ISIS rhetoric to bring an end to Sykes Picot will not materialise as distinct groups of:

Arabia at first wandering tribes have migrated between Iraq and Syria and ruled by distinct powers. Many scholars believe that ISIS desire to erase Sykes Picot is rooted in imaginations, rather than turning it into a reality, as history, truth regards, to it, has already been made.

Arabia was united under Mohammed in ancient times, but the expansion of Islam out of the Arabian Peninsula brought divisions between groups that did not sit comfortably one with the other. Under the Ottoman empire, there was some sense of unity in the Arab world, whilst geographically the regions or states were under secularity run independent governments.

Iraq and Syria have failed to come together as a single caliphate in the past, and the ISIS state will not fail to achieve its good, albeit it has tried to exploit the weaknesses in Iraq's government since the Iraq war and equally the lawlessness created in both nations, by the terror groups and civil war, the fall of Saddam Hussein government and the near collapse of the Assad region.

The ISIS state does not recognise or wish to reorganise the Sykes Picot agreement and the development of Iraq and Syria as two separate nations, coming up to a full century,

The legitimacy of the status quo is placed under question, and scrutiny but an alternative to it is no more legitimate or stabilising for the region. The common perception in international relations communities is that artificial borders create fragmented nations, and such artificial borders over time lead to conflicts and this is a common theme in nations that have artificially created, such as India and Pakistan, Israel and Gaza and economies fail due to unrest sectarian divisions, boundaries of nations, which have formed naturally without conflict, based on geographical division do not manifest these factors have a strong sense of nationality and belonging and lend themselves to being more stable.

Often race goes with geographical terrain i.e., the indigenous peoples of the lands. The making of artificial political frontiers and boundaries, results in artificial geographical cohesion and territorial integrity.

The Middle east internal strife is mainly due to powerful religious differences, the need to gain more land, expand and due to increase in internal populations.

The animosity between different religions is extreme and this is evident in the Arabian Peninsula. Artificial states disregard first in time so first in right doctrines or legitimate prior claims on the territories.

Natural states do not have problems of authenticity, legitimacy, or natural identity, and groups or peoples with sense of national identity have no motivation so either identify or behave like natural citizens.

Syria's borders have become porous and have been infiltrated during the conflict equally gas and oil trade has created foreign international zones within the country. Kurds feel no belonging to any nation, due to their past historic experience – Turkey, Syria and Iraq and have inhabited all three as transnational peoples. Economic cooperation is the only way forward to bring peace to these nations instead of political violence.

It is an instrument of peace, and brings people close to further the region and a common purpose economic interest in Syria's energy resource and markets has encouraged outside nations to be freed to ensure Syria's stability. Like Syria the Palestine conflict of 2013, was due to a dispute regarding territory, stemming from a decision by the United Nations to divide it into two zones, Jewish and Arabian.

Once Palestine was part of the Ottoman empire, and mainly Jews and Arabs inhabited that land for a few centuries.

The Jewish presence was a minor one, only 25, /30,000 people and the Zionist movement out of Europe began as early as 1882, to consolidate European Jews as migrants to their holy lands.

The Arabs were resistant to Zionists, Jews claim to their lands, and flet their sovereignty was being challenged by- a hostile alien presence, which was beginning to impose their will on them. Israel's occupation of Palestine segments and Golan heights of Syria escalated into a six-day war and escalating conflicts ever since then.

The seizure of Arab land became an issue and was deemed immoral by the entire Arab world and countries like Jordan, Egypt, Syria and Iraq were the first to voice their vehement opposition against it.

DIPLOMACY IRAN, IRAQ, KURDS, SYRIA OIL AND GAS.

The loss of sovereign territory violated the core beliefs of the Arabs and was seen as a major violation of their Peninsula.

Many negotiations for a deal failed to satisfy both nationalists. The same problem arose with the Kurds unilateral declaration of autonomy in the northeastern part of the country as this area contains Syria's vast oil and gas resources and lands of great economic significance and importance.

Post Iraq, the Kurds pursued financial freedom, gaining special autonomy via the Kurdish government, in one of the richest Dohuk, Ebril, awash with oil resources and refineries as well as in SulayanI, Yah. Turkey was quick to seize opportunity and struck a deal that would allow oil to be diverted and transported to Turkey, from this newly acquired Kurdish region and that all finances were to be deposited in Kurdish bank accounts in Turkey. A revenue sharing a budget plan was drawn up between the Turkey government and the Kurds.

The deal thus ensures for the key profits in energy and Kurds gain recognition from the international nations. The Kurds although not a state, will have earned in excess of some twenty billion from Iraq. In time Kurds will seek Kurdistan as they grow financially stronger and will not wish to remain part of Ira enriched by the oil region of Iraq.

Thus, the oil economic co-operation between turkey as part of the NATO ally and on the European mainland Kurdistan and Iraq will become an economic model and a fluid status not requiring political borders as Sykes Picot post the wars in 1947.

A balance of stability in the region is the optimal solution in Arabia thus reducing aggression internally and externally to other Arab nations.

Foreign nations and international oil investors have created peace for both Syria and Iraq, with Kurds as vital to this process and for international cooperation. The Arab states are already too weak to maintain borders crisis in the region and state falling, collapsing and facing future failures.

For the Nasser Model of united Arab nations, the entire Arabian Peninsula would need to undergo major transformation and create a dual system or hybrid of monarchies dynasties combined to people's chaotic leaders, this could be a sustainable form or hybrid approach in line with Kingdom religious style Arab governance and ideologies.

The Gulf and energy policy depends now on the end of the wars in Syria, Yemen, Iraq, Libya, or for the dust to settle from conflicts since 2001 to 2019. The setbacks suffered for the normalisation of Israel and Bahrain's problems and the various issues rejig the sharp focus back on the main and fundamental US—Saudi relations.

The Military-and security policies, the peace process initiatives, the policies on terrorism and proliferation have faded into the background once Iran came to the fore as an international issue, under the Trump administration, and became mainstay- for academics, international law scholars, foreign policy advisers, and Middle east politics experts. It seems it will remain for the future as no conclusion is in sight.

IV IRAN DIPLOMACY AND THE IMPACT ON THE ARABIAN PENINSULA AND MNE'S IRAN AND AFRICA DIPLOMACY

Iran studied Africa in great depth and understood as scholarship that Conflicts and MNE's and Oil and gas go hand in hand, so do fragile environments. The lists of places where MNE's operate are also places, where there is the maximum number of conflicts. The list of ongoing conflicts in Africa are immense, and lists major nations and minor, such as Egypt, Sudan, Libya, Tunisia, Algeria, Morocco, Somalia, Uganda, Mali, Mauritania, Niger, Nigeria, Western Sahara, democratic republic of Congo and Chad, as well as the more publicised conflicts of the Middle East, Israeli Palestine, North Africa and Afghanistan. However, these places are of great human interest for a myriad of reasons, but especially due to its tremendously rich natural wildlife, ranging from Lions, Wilder beast Leopards, Rhino, Giraffe, Chimpanzees, to name but a few. The environmental issues are caused by several effects in the African natural environment and have impact on all forms of natural life and their fragile habitats. There are concerns about desertification, the splitting of the African continent at its ridges, water supplies shortage, population explosions, and flora and fauna depletion. Besides desertification, there is deforestation, soil degradation and enhanced air pollution, due to drilling, logging and mining over the decades if not more.

Several debates over the past decade have raged over multinational corporations, and their global outreach and how they must be regulated.

This question Iran and its diplomatic tradecraft answer and understand well, and its challenges and key questions, have centred on governance models and to connect theory and policy into the practical field within which they operate. The biggest multinationals have been in the news in the recent years, are oil conglomerates and multinational entities.

Several theoretic propositions have been subject to reviews, new analysis and further analysis and developments of these have resulted in recommendations, policies, codes, rules via, key European, British, American and international institutions, thus updating old regulations, into the new.

Over the past decade, the spread of American corporations, have generated models and fresh governance features and soon these ideas have become globalised, and some have been inexorable.

MNE corporate governance, is now understood through the manner in which finance companies, lend to them, how these same companies, are directed controlled and how investors in MNE's hope to get a return for their investments. Institutional investors constantly seek to diverse risk and wish to take advantage of the oil companies, for their growth in fertile lands and which offer considerable growth opportunities through constantly emerging markets.

The end of Gaddafi's 42-year rule in Libya ended abruptly. Everyone was concerned about the fate of Libya, a rich oil producing nation, its peoples and the goal was to develop into a peaceful prosperous and free nation, it deserved to be. Iran understood this, having been engaged with Russia and Lebanon in Syria rescue. Bodies such as OECD, have been active since Libya and other conflicts, stock markets so reliant on company performance have been publishing new corporate governance rules to promote knowledge as well as to bring about awareness to enable investors to feel secure whilst taking on risks. The question of corporate governance work continues through established committees in the USA, EU and the international bodies. Thus compliance, to codes is important and thus inform on shareholder values. However, the future of Libya has never been under threat. The United States lacks a clear policy and strategy towards Libya, which makes the debate corporate governance and stakeholder enablement much timelier.

The nature and function of global companies in global markets in varying jurisdictions must understand these codes, be willing to comply, and Iran as a global oil power, knows this as do Syria and Iraq, thus irrespective of the nature and function of their corporations. This shift in paradigm of governance and awareness has general and specific advantages for all parties including the companies themselves and investors, and thus, more capital can be exploited, thus equity bringing fresh advantages for their sphere of business. The focus is on the policy in Libya, Syria, Iraq, Yemen, and their current situation, where partners of the USA want to work with the Libyan people, into a smooth transition. This involves the oil companies and the larger corporations, and MNE's operating in places like Libya.

The right forms of rules, codes, Iran knows as do all oil nations, for their own company regulations, and to enhance greater foreign and local investment. However, the regulations or codes demand for obvious-s reasons, greater transparency and thus transform sluggish powers into efficient organisations and Iran had witnessed along with Saudi Arabia, corrupt practices being changed by regulation.

It is important for nations to have investor protection to enable the expansion of already existing capital markets. Libya does not rank in the top tier of issues that currently impact US priorities in the Middle east and Iran saw the instability growing in the Gulf post Libya and Iraq. However, company reform continues as part of diplomatic structures, regardless of Jurisdiction, where there has been a conflict and where there are vast oil reserves. Company structure and function reform needs to encompass both reform in how companies function but equally- for expansion of financial markets, to enhance foreign investment protection.

Expansion of financial capital markets means the need to move away from concentrated power in company governance but to allocate this power to investors too, and equally restructuring claims from private customers in a global or financial crisis. All these Iran knew are the makeup of the region, in Africa Libya remains central due to its nexus of geography, terrorism and most importantly its oil and gas energy systems.

Success breeds more success, and thus expanding into foreign jurisdictions, can be simplified if there are uniform rules, regulations, directives, and recommendations and simplified as codes.

The shift from a pessimistic future to optimism is necessary as recent decades have shown that the stock exchange has been unstable, at best and erratic at worst. The Model of capitalism has taken a profound beating. The dot.com bubble burst a long time ago.

Libya impacts the Mediterranean, Tunisia and Egypt, and has become since 2016, energy oil and gas active, providing 1.3 million barrels of oil per day to the global market. Oil companies and the collapse of Enron began a different cycle highlighting that greed was consuming these companies as doubt exceeded the binary code evolution.

The economic cycles could not understand that shareholders creditors, employees, suppliers, customers, clients, subsidiary companies, need to widen the chief concepts of MNE governance, in order to breed success continually. The fallout from conflicts, economic collapses, was a shock to their systems, and the markets and economies felt the pressure created by the collapse? This created new stresses on the models of MNE governance and stock markets struggled and even failed to return themselves to stable, failing to deliver. These tangible events, added to the emerging list of concerns and the dominant American model had to return to the drawing board to devise more paradigms. Theories were devised to reverse failures to successes again.

Iran knew Libya serves as a key port of migration between Africa and Europe. A stable Libya with a fully functioning government could provide the same for Tunisia and Egypt and contribute stability to the African nations as a whole. Since the start of the conflicts in oil jurisdictions significant steps were taken with the Sarbanes Oxley act, and convergence boards were active, as were coordinating groups on auditing control issues.

The new government were formed on either side of the Atlantic post the start of the Middle east conflicts and fresh revenues were announced in response to global disasters in trade and industry. The competitiveness of the American economy, in the context of global trades emerging markets and overseas growth resulted in the models' expressing realities on multiple levels and now modern giants would have to incorporate all influences in their paradigms. In the UK several reviews were made and set up to establish norms for big companies these companies were in all nations of the Gulf, and also to review company law as it stands. How should the scope of law be extended thus imparting governance of MNE's that spanned multiple jurisdictions.

Reviews were fed in by large amount of information, several academic reports reached Iran and all over the world, on oil companies and their structure function, extensive law economics literature surveys made on all manner of legal issues were noted that could arise influence and impact new paradigms – various business research centres, legal bodies became involved as did Iranian with stakeholder employee issues, client co-partnerships, shareholder employees issues, client co-partnerships, shareholders, representation and co-determination, were introduced to make sure MNE governance in the new forms had installed within it board structures that were efficient, transparency and accountability and that these would be compatible with novel concepts now evolving.

From the onset of Libya's transition in 2012, US policy has been to support UNSMIL (United nations, support mission in Libya) and Gulf countries) and to guide them through elections, several transitional governments and peace initiatives.

The department of economic affairs, trade and industry, department of trade, became busy. Reviewing company law, legislation, paradigms, governance, represent the only unique way to formulate fresh policies and to see if what applied to a given jurisdiction could then be transported as a stock market model. New models, had to be aware of intense, and growing global competitiveness, the impact of global market forces on these new company concerns and widening interests in the Arabian Peninsula and Iran.

In the aftermath of the Benghazi tragedy, the Trump administration has tried to invigorate Libya's transition, there are many economic challenges, and preventing the sale of oil outside the national system, since July 2011-2019.

All these Iran built into its constraints on key proposals such that concrete workable legislation resulting from intelligent and abstract but well developed, thesis and theories.

How does the MNE legislations address the key issues post the 9/11 conflicts, the collapse of Enron and dot.com companies, conflicts and if it should be amended in the light of ever-growing concerns from around the world. These concerns had to be acknowledged and converted into the right agreements which could produce the correct thesis and their development in turn would manifest as practical solutions.

The debate was both developed in the USA along with the UK who rejected certain considerations, on the grounds that they did not stand up, to the standards of scrutiny and often failed for ideological or economic reasons.

Iranian scholars studied the models, the Model of an MNE and thereby its administration and control, have been developed over decades if not more, with built in practical legal principles, practice procedures, experience of directors and thus have evolved on the criteria of theoretical, ethical and practical reasoning, and through economic equations, to account for the general and specific nature of firms and thus serve as anchors and guiding principles for future growth. Theories based on a firm thesis result in influential foundations, for near future developments, but bearing in mind, the specific issues of the company, how it wishes to lead in global markets, and therefore how it wishes to govern its principle and minor structures and dissimilar jurisdictions, Iran had no problem embracing these with other nations and companies as its paradigm of diplomacy.

The US Policy was for example to acknowledge Haftar's role in securing Libya's oil, and to support his allies in Cairo, Abu Dhabi and Riyadh and thus a more intense level of engagement with Libya the Gulf nations and the oil and gas MNE's that operate there. These are everyday challenges in the Gulf regions post the end of wars.

The amendments, adjustments, before they are made, would question the basic concepts such as what truly constitutes an MNE in Gulf regions, how has it been formed, and how it conducts its business, function, form, and what are the nature of its transactions, where are they made and held. Which global markets in the Gulf has the firm or firms, emerged in, and what are its hierarchical structures, the goods it produces, and the mechanisms it uses to establish its authority, relationships in markets, how do its array of contracting behaviours perform with efficiency and can these be enhanced, producing greater profitability with more enhanced efficiency and not disturbing the Gulf regions. The firm thus could perform better if all singular individual contract terms, relations, were entered in as a multi layered mechanism such as price, production costs, remunerations, limits and this could apply to all contracts made for the supply of the same foods or services. This would provide a degree of certainty for the nations in which it operates as wealth creation, for both short, medium and long-term contracts and would create direction, to both the firm and its customers as the firm evolves in different jurisdictions.

The nature of the firm must fit its existential reality, and its contracts nexus relating to the supply of services, or goods, must result in reduced cost of weighing in longer terms. Contracts which are ineffective, to series of mild or short-term contracts in the gulf regions, which do not conform to the concept of certainty lends itself to fostering dominance, authority in a given sphere, as well as better relationships, with other companies, subsidiaries, clients and employers.

The brand and essence of the company is thus promoted in the Gulf as oil and gas, by distinguishing itself through long term contractual relationships rather than shorter midterm ones, in market fields its exists and enters to establish and explore. When theories are realistic and sound, policies ensure a better ongoing authority through which exchanges can be done. There has to be continued experimentation till equilibrium is reached between market and organisation.

It was clear to Iran, that arrangements by economists and jurists alike that amendments to codes that govern policy and legislation with regards to companies, should limit modifications that could have a deleterious effect on costs i.e. there should be no onerous burdens placed on companies to be effective at growing their local or global gulf business. The MNE must retain its direction and not lose sight of it, and equally maintain its authority in its chosen field is essential and this characterises all firms operating in Gulf nations.

Governance must be exercised within the firm and out with it i.e., in the market in exactly the same way especially in Gulf nations, Iran, Syria, Iraq, Libya, African nations as Nigeria and Niger delta. Governance must be exercised within the firm and out with it i.e., in the market in exactly the same way. Thus, the firm has redress to courts if problems arise and their inputs and outputs can be critically discerned over monthly and final year basis.

Gulf global company's organisations have to be streamlined, whether they are in the Gulf region, Africa or North Africa, equally if they are in Mexico, Scotland and England or in other key parts of the world.

Efficiency in organizing is key to success and metrics weigh in heavily. Productivity and efficiency are the rewards for adaptations and productivity creates its own rewards for adaptations, and productivity creates its own rewards in time, as understood by key economic doctrines.

For global organisations to work efficiently, the people that makeup the system are vital, and the inputs and outputs are measured with reference to them, as individuals and within teams how they perform.

However, for MNE governance, for it to be precise, mathematically, efficient and skilled, must have a way of measuring individual performance, contribution and thus once gauged, to reward this for even greater productivity.

Monitoring performance in multiple jurisdictions comes at a cost, and parameters which kick in matters, with sensitive relations among nations they matter even more, if rules are not obeyed or shirked, on board this can stifle productivity, and the risk of greater competition is more from rival firms such as Russian or Indian or even Chinese.

Within the organisation, a team member can be assigned the task of monitoring performance of its members, but there are always the inherent risks too. The task can be complex, and privileges abound for functions motivation and sufficiency. Thus, centralising monitoring can be proactive and can tease out problems enhanced by low productivity and in time rather than relying on the market; performance is key monitor for MNE team productivity. No centralised, arrangement thus is less in formative and thus the analysis can be applied to different organisations.

Ownership can be diverse, in that there can be many stakeholders each one owning a small part of the firm and complications in Gulf nations as Iran knows are complex these can enter in due to shareholders, demanding that every decision needs their approval, or that they are informed about, such creating further costs on an ongoing basis rather the cost of a single bad decision that results in costs insured. To prevent, this, decisions are normally made by a small group of managers and who oversee most major decisions, structure and function of the firm and even if it needs to be dissolved.

The MNE governance rules, recommend, these specific arrangements as essential and thus giving shareholders rights and flexibility to see or retain share, if bad decisions affect them, adversely or if they feel that they are unable to influence key decisions.

There are implications and Iran and Gulf nations know this that for such forms of flexible governance structures, as there are external management groups and at times, with diversification, these influences can come together as forces to weaken or even displace central management structures in a precise and very active way. The emergences of these forms arise due to the doctrine of delegated authority now entrenched in the firms' systems.

The corporations in foreign jurisdictions can act, as a specialised market within its own right, and owners are seen as chief or residual claimants of the same. Employees are by all accounts not involved in decision making and this would be contrary to common economic logic.

Thus, ownership and control should be separated, and direction is best achieved in Gulf Libya or Iran as nations, through diplomacy as directors and equally shareholders. Thus, separation of powers, explains the new forms of efficient organisation, with the paradigm of business, contracts and products in one marketplace. Equally ownership in Gulf nations has complexities as an MNE deals with business, control and capital. Thus, the various factors within an organisation are owned by a set of principles. Thus, the firm dwells within a plethora of contracts created through inputs and outputs, and the receipts are thus distributed or shared as rewards – The Gulf nations in Arabia have long-standing relations with Oil and Gas companies. Ownership is thus complicated by claims that a firm is owed by lenders, but a firm cannot be attached to a false notion as MNE's decisions are only the produce of the owners.

Concepts of management, and risk bearing are distinct as one deals with managing and motivating towards peak performance, and the other which studies the market to exploit opportunities which although may result in growth may have in built risk which would need to be appraised. Shareholders however minimise risk by owning a portfolio of shares and the owner manager invest all their capital in the one single firm.

Thus shareholders, investors, owners have different perspectives to risks, and the bearing of gain over losses. The capital markets send out signals which impact how management is performing. This in turn can add extra pressure on the firms and performance related pay and other issues arise as a consequence. The board of directors can include managers who may need to be disciplined for poor market performance and thus Gulf nations are able to choose the best, and the inherent flaws in structure and function of firms must meet the expectations of Gulf nations as global organisations. External directors do play a role and are a mechanism which can prevent hostile takeovers in the face of poor market performance. Shareholders do not step in to oversee either performance risk or poor management structures in the firm. It is clear that shareholders are not owners of the firm, as they are out with the management structure as are lenders and security holders. It is clear that establishing the inner workings of the firm and outer workings too are essential in defining what constitutes a firm or a global organisation in Gulf nations, and what diplomatic structures are placed in them for smooth operations.

Thus, this perspective model for a firm place, the nexus of contractual obligations as key to its functioning place aside social responsibility and its focus is primarily on a firm operating in global markets. This governance of an organisation is tied up with the governance of its business contracts.

Certain aspects thus become expanded with respect to functions in organisational governance. The classic literature too focuses on the firm as property, the rights reserved in the owner both in terms of business, capital and human assets, thus this too can be developed on this basis on the separation of power arrangement.

Thus, models of governance, whatever the view of what constitutes a MNE should be to increase productivity and not upset incentive structures. Thus, it seems there are many stakeholders in a firm and equally in its growing structure. This concept is not new but has been reconceptualised many times. Can this be extended to include managers, community, employers, customers, suppliers, owners and shareholders.

The great Jurist Kant's principles come into play in that MNE's should be managed and conducted in the interest of all, and thus director responsibility, duty of care and that the environment and the least of the stakeholders must benefit from the decisions. Goodwill is an important part and to perform with a duty of care. How can this be integrated in diverse jurisdictions from Africa to Australia to the Middle east is the next question.

Iran had to ask many questions, who then are the stakeholders and how does a corporation transaction costs and incentives work by incorporating external stakeholders. Is there a problem with interference? What are the mechanisms by which stakeholders' interests should or not be taken into consideration. There is a doctrine of stakeholder enabling principle which activates but can be constrained by the narrow definition of what constitutes a stakeholder, is narrow and rigidly construed.

There are many types of stakeholders, environmentalists, business, core strategy developers, formal and informal those with business relationships with the company. There are however stakeholders who are key to the success and survival of the firm in the Gulf regions.

The firms operating in Iran and other nations in the Gulf requires stakeholders, in new jurisdictions, hostile environments in the context of threats that may arise, or they are confronted with and also to establish the business. The Firm's business environment includes all those connected within and without the business and who are all those connected within and without the business and who are all adherents of the firm. There is often a flux between the categories of stakeholders, who can move themselves in a manner that changes their nature, legitimacy and balance of power, and complexities can arise within and through various definitions and their extrapolations. Thus, different interests can surface, and classifications enable the management of these and how these should be addressed. However, directors must carry out their obligations in an ethical way.

But how can this ethical responsibility be enforced in multiple jurisdictions, in war zones, in hostile environments, in nations with laws at dissonance with the company's Should the MNE follow a social good model, be a trusteeship and transcend its definitions as those pertaining only to binding contracts. Thus, directors could be overseers as trustees too, look after the interests of the company, both tangible and intangible and this this role would be mutually exclusive from the agent role responsible for its shareholders. The long-established business, with trust relationships is an evolutionary thing but companies have to always be careful of external forces infiltrating or of hostile takeovers.

Thus, balancing interests, involvement, decision making, are issues, which need to be addressed by company directors, to resolve the future of stakeholders, and whether or not they should have an active role in the company. Rawls and Kant two eminent jurists of natural justice would have suggested that the correct approach is to be, ethically responsible and engaging with stakeholders in the environment as a just process. What would be the rights and responsibilities of directors, shareholders, individually and within groups? So how does this serve the company's interest as a strategy to maximise different interests of stakeholders within the company's environments.

Thus, excesses of big MNE's and corporations can be checked and balanced by stakeholders, and this is a departure from traditional concepts into the realms of social and intuitive appeal of marrying business overreach and to alter the dominant status quo. Within these new nuances new constants and variables emerge and will have to be addressed.

Transaction cost economics as an economic doctrine, suggests that for governance to work well, that suppliers and financiers should be first as stakeholders, but should they have a part in controlling the company. The best thing stakeholders can do is secure their stake. Capital too should be entered and embedded into the protective governance structures.

Company law reviews of MNE's and corporation law and management, their relationships are the main issue, determine a company's directing and prospects in new environments. A universal code or rules, to mix the two would be ideal. Practice codes are preferred to legislation as regulatory paradigms and thus targets can be reached.

Yemen on the 19th of March 2015, US-UK-Saudi Arabia, and eight other nations, led intervention began when the Arab spring, and civil war erupted, the same as in Libya and Syria. There were too many belligerents vying for state power. US led intervention under Obama administration and latterly Trump's began on the 24th of March 2015. The eight states in the coalition with them joined them against the Houthis, bombing their positions, in Sana and a joint statement by the nations of the Oil Gulf nations, the Gulf cooperation council was made, excluding Oman, that they intervened against the Houthi's in Yemen at the request of the Hadi's government, and thus Barack Obama, backed the Saudi Arabian nation, to declare the control of Yemeni airspace. The drone strikes, continued till as late as 8th January 2019, whilst the world focused on the Syrian civil war, the more interesting of the two, Yemen, Nigeria, and Libya were forgotten. There was no resolution, and CNN reports stated that 10, 160, 000 Yemenis had been displaced and become refugees due to the conflict from March 2015 to January 2019.

Yemen's export goods include mainly crude oil, and it is like no other Arab nation, Iraq, Syria, Libya, all oil and gas producers – but Yemen, is not represented at the OPEC exploring nations. Yemen has proven crude oil reserves of more than 4 billion barrels, MNE's first arrived in Yemen in 1982 in the south and found an oil base near Marib in 1984. A total of some 800,000 barrels of oil per day were produced in 1995, and MNE's oil refineries began operations, and Russians too discovered, Shabwah, Europeans, MNE's discovered, oil from Malta, in the Hadhramaut, as early as 1993, and production levels reached as high as 542,000 barrels per day as early as 1999, and production levels reached as high as 542,000 barrels per day as early as 1999. New fins were discovered in Jinnah, formerly known as the Joint oil exploration area and near East Shabwah blocks. Yemen oil exports earned millions than latterly in excess of US dollars 1.75 billion.

Total multinational corporation of France signed agreement with Yemeni government, for the export of natural gas and the investments made by France were to cover a period of a minimum of twenty-five years.

Thus, a common theme emerges that throughout oil basin regions conflicts have now become dominant features, Nigeria, Yemen, Libya, African nations and Arab. Multinational companies along with governments had to operate there and corporate governance alongside these multiple factors operating had to be viewed afresh and doctrines created, and company law rules modified in keeping with this violent status.

Legislation, however, oversees the fiduciary duty and duty of care required of directors. US government, UK law commission have placed these duties on a statutory footing for now.

Duty of care was a quagmire, Iran knew this but what should be this duty of care, should it extend only to company interests or to the environment in which they operate and even the wider community. Whose interest should be considered, what should be the priority of these interests and what legal mechanism should be deployed to achieve these ends. Thus in law, the function and management of companies, is essential for the benefit of its shareholders, but it is also for the benefit of stakeholders, the community in which it resides, functions and does its business accounting and disclosure requirements of the company are necessary as are the interests of those that fund and finance the company. There should as the Jurists Rawls and Kant would have expounded there should be two principles fully engaged not just to maximise welfare of its environment and stakeholders. But critics suggest that the two are incompatible principles, and maximisation of shareholder value will impact on the maximization of welfare, and this has been evidenced in various jurisdictions where MNE's operate.

Thus, the company law frameworks emphasise key principles and cover all of director's responsibilities and while establishing success, in foreign jurisdiction for the shareholders al l other relevant considerations mut be keyed in, Public listed companies hold real economic and commercial power and operate with the same affecting billions of lives. They are and must by law be directed to publish their annual operating and financial reports, thus covering their governance and transactional features. Everything that is material must therefore be included in the assessment performance real and projected, views of users, prospects for the future, impact on the indigenous communities and environments.

How should policing managerial discretion for negative effects or through competitiveness, potential conflicts, complications, between it and its society's shareholders, directors, be viewed and the obligations met by directors through its given pluralism? Iran pondered, could Director's duties thus codified, is it possible to take the various principles, be included in a model, and the ethical ones too, as well as the commercial duties such as the honest exercise of discretion, purpose, decision making, in good faith, under all circumstances, and taking on board all consequences of his acts whilst promoting success and objectives of the company for the benefits of its environment and members as a whole – skill care, fostering relationships, with employees, suppliers, clients and to understand the impact of its operations.

Within given environments is short, to maintain the reputation as cited by the high standards of business conduct. It must therefore be included in its policies environmental issues; comply with relevant laws and regulations. The list can be exhaustive and can be amended whilst reviewing procedures where appropriate. It should be noted that although it is possible for companies to deny real problems exist, there are reasonable ways to consider facts and information. Account must be taken of any improbable contingency that may overweigh benefits and amendments to clauses in review documents can be done to deal with it. Arbitration is a way forward to deal with altered values and clauses in variables as they arise.

Rationality must be used so there is no neglect in evaluation of constants and variables due to the deficit in the clauses of a contract. The primary goal of a multinational corporation is to protect its integrity and therefore diffusion of power is implicit in this objective and alignment of wealth production, human capital and assets, and to prevent, conflicts among shareholders and stakeholders alike such that terror and fear does not paralyse and destroy the firm. These are then some of the questions, answers that have been energised due to the structure and function of MNE's themselves.

Thus, stakeholder enablement will help many communities and nations, or multiple jurisdictions, in which the Major Oil corporations establish themselves and work. A clear example is of West Africa, Nigeria and the Niger Delta. Everyone has heard of Sara O Wiwa who was a tribal chief in Nigeria and an oil and gas activist, known for his environmental safety of indigenous African communities. His Nigerian environmental activism was well known by directors of oil companies operating there such as Shell and BP, as well as other notable ones. Saro Wiwa's son had the returned to Africa out of a sense of duty, and gratitude after the loss of his father. Historians had begun to study the plight of the Ogoni people and media had become active. Advisers had arrived in Port Harcourt and other parts of Nigeria. The solo political structure although very complex had changed. Tribe and class distinctions had not vanished in Port Harcourt and there were those who thought themselves super citizens or classified others as being so. In this part of Africa Goerge Orwell, would have been right when he had stated that some would always be more equal than others.

Kemule Ken Beeson, Saro Wiwa was an environmental activist for many years He was executed along with ten other defendants after a mock trial by the Nigerian government of the time, of 1995, outside the Shell camp. He was a member of the Ogoni people, and he had been followed by the media by great interest. He was an ethnic Nigerian and belonged to a minority group and had taken up the cause of the Ogoni land in the Niger delta, which had been targeted for crude oil extraction since the 1950's and had suffered extreme and unmediated environmental damage. He had devoted his life to human rights and environmental causes and particularly in Ogoni land and he was the instigator of the movement for the survival of the Ogoni peoples.

He advocated widely for the Ogoni bill of rights and started a movement setting out his demands that included increased autonomy for the Ogoni people, a fair share pf the proceeds of oil extraction by the multinationals, remediation of environmental damage, to their lands and other issues of human interest. However, his voice was stifled in Nigeria but heard by the rest of the world. He was undermined and jailed for several months at a time. Later four Ogoni chiefs were brutally murdered. Saro Wiwa, was denied entry on the day of the murders and he was arrested for incitement to hatred against them.

He did not receive a fair trial but a mock one, with false witnesses. He was accused and an indictment brough against him on criminal charges. Sao wiwa, claimed his innocence till the very end but he was hanged at the hands of his own countrymen, Nigerian military personnel. There was international outrage, but it came too late. His sons won his case, in America and a book was published by him entitled in the shadow of a saint, a son's journey in understanding his father's legacy.

The Ogoni people continue with their struggles and agonies and various crisis have been precipitated in oil rich Nigeria since then. Saro-Wiwa was the hero of the region and had been awarded the Goldman environmental prize. After his death the world had been up in arms and sanctions had been in place for three and a half years against the government of Nigeria. His son's case against Shell had resulted in substantial award for damages. A timely and compelling event and report filed with surprising and inconvenient observations about the plight of oil rich Africa with the globalisation of commerce and the part played by multinationals such as Shell and British petroleum across various jurisdictions in the world, conducting extensive oil extractions and oil and gas explorations and their impact on the indigenous populations has been down played, till the event of the death of Sao Wiwa came to light.

The criticism of the Ogoni people has been noted by the media where they condemn MNE's who exploit indigenous differences for violent gains, but praise leaders who act as trustees, looking after stakeholders in an ethical way, and include them according the stakeholder enablement principles set out in the combined codes for international and national corporate governance.

Equally they praise those that seek to harness the values of Africanism, Arabian or even red Indian values in America, and keep their environment safe, whilst entering their jurisdictions, to harness oil and seek wealth, the call for bold African Arabian leadership to rein in the many tribes and religious rivalries and lay the ground for a new economic political consensus, based on evolving corporate laws is the way forward.

The Ogoni people defy conventional wisdom, and their leaders suggest that African Arabian religion and beliefs and politics are inseparable, and their partnership needs to be harnessed under the Stakeholder enabling principles.

However, there are other issues in Nigeria and Niger delta in that the Islamic state ISWAP also known as Jamad -Wahl Jihad is a Jihadist terrorist organisation, based in northeastern Nigeria, also active in Port Harcourt, Lagos, Cameroon, Benin, Niger Delta, and other places in west Africa.

It was founded by Mohammed Yusef and aligned with the Islamic state of Iraq and levant – (ISIS and ISIL), tens of thousands have been killed almost 2.3 million have been displaced from their homes and it is ranked the world's deadliest by the global terrorist index. The ISWAP is responsible for military forces, suppression, summary executions of leaders and is known to be increasingly sophisticated against soft targets, including suicide bombings and targeting multinational oil companies, buildings are responsible for beheadings, murder, hijackings, of local and foreign workers in Nigeria.

The famous Baga massacre, attrition of Christian and catholic diocese, Daphi kidnappings, Dalori attack, Maiduguri attack, Operation, Lafiay Dole, attacks all over Nigeria, killing and massacre of Nigerian soldiers, kidnapping for ransom, extortion, are some citations of terrorism for ISWAP many are not recorded or known.

Amidst this environment the stakeholder enabling principle, directors duties, became dominant and codes have to be applied, with extreme caution, discretion and discernment – bearing in mind the safety of the ordinary indigenous tribes and distinguishing them from malafide groups in the region and yet maintaining ethical conduct towards the fragile environment surrounding their oil and gas operations.

DIALOGUE OF CHRIST AS ROMAN ZEUS WITH SOLUS CHRISTOS

THE PRINCIPLE OF JUST WARS

A moral principle, a moral corrector, a morality-based war, signal and response, Christ to Christos Arabia was the great setting of a climactic battlefield and became an epic battle lasting a quarter of a century, the battle of all battles – the longest, vastest, greatest epic war a Soul war, a Solus war, between moral right and moral wrong, a first mythical and original battle in the modern world, post Napoleonic, two world wars, myriad pacific wars, in the intervening time, leading and culminating in the longest war of the human time line.

It is an epic war now virtually every child knows it. The temperament and temper of the story is, however, otherworldly, as classic made contemporary.

It is perhaps the greatest literature, and nothing compared to it, its breadth, depth, characterisation, guile and now has a place among the great and epic literary original works in the contemporary history of the world.

There is a sudden signal from space, an aviator a Christ perhaps, a Sagittarius an Alpha roman god christos, Zeus or Solus, the signal is transduced and received by a minor solus, who then responds as a signal response transduction, through the airwaves.

CHRIST BEGINS TO SIGNAL TO CHRISTOS, THE SUN AS IT WERE SPEAKING TO A MINOR SUN.

You are about to engage in a battle, to defend morality, on earth, you are no ordinary god, you are the reincarnation of returning souls a solus, the aspect who fosters, preserves, the world against the forces constantly working to destroy and corrupt it, you as solus have entered earth in many guises, as the heir apparent, from the chambers of the Christ, thus in you are vested the powers of earthly majesty and supreme cosmic powers. You have shown me you are worthy, the one vested with the powers to destroy evil and protect all good. Everyone will gather but the laurel is yours and yours alone, the silence falls like a lull before a storm, this is no genial hour of song and rhyme, but for the growth of time, the shadows hear your footsteps, and the air knows you are here again. The war about to begin is no one's property, but as a combatant, you are driven a glorious warrior, this is your victory, you are the motivator, encourager, the promise of Christ, there is this mighty army assembled, heroic warriors great and gifted, the declaration of war will begin and the drums and cavalry will be informed. The night skies will go on and on, for days and days, till the roar of the coming war will spread far and wide. The sound of a response, a tumultuous sound will echo throughout the earth and the heavens.

Everything is impermanent, only the universal part of you is indestructible. The Self remains untouched, is eternal, immutable, the cause for war remains you cannot draw back now, there is a supreme good, a higher cause that persuades and propels us, this is part of illumination – the storm is raging all around us, the clouds of judgement are propelling us on, the rivers flow only in one direction, from the river to the sea, remember you are an immortal, soul, the soul is everything, while you dwell on your immediate predicaments. Rewards follow you through lifetimes, not all cause and effect are painful, it can be very fruitful, knowledge is power, enhanced perception is key, but it must be used wisely. All are driven to action, there can be no avoidance, as long as it engages the forces of evolution the action is needed, you will establish good on earth, the purpose of life is not the same for everyone, that distinguishes them and the distinctions that are above, must match those below, although here is action, there is inaction, and between these man and woman dwell. Selfless service is the highest sacrifice, the goal to reach the highest step in the ladder of self, by all and everyone, by all means possible, once established then you are in effect invincible.

RESPONSE SOLUS

Thank you, O Christ, the sun of all suns, life is taken so much for granted, an evolving cycle, a positive cycle, or several cycles, and paradigms, are generated. The rose in bloom unaffected by the thorns around you, a lily floating on water clear or unclear, the consciousness its 12 gates, or portals to our higher selves, they come and go, he who has conquered first himself can conquer the world, to thine self be always true, never deny it, for the self directs and knows the reasons, the realms of the righteous await us those countless lifetimes, there are two natures in us, you and me, one is all the body, and its attachments, make up the world you live in then there is a second nature your cosmic nature, one you are born with which grows the same, thus like colossus you and I abide in two worlds, at once, the goal being to gain our full personhood, here on earth. The first nature can purify the second nature, and enlighten it, the inner world can fling world upon world, of outer worlds, but the power of this belongs to the inner life, of soul and solus, the sun within, the consciousness directs itself into the self, which directs it to attain the supreme goal to move to the next destination at will, or return back to the same one, the first honour is between cold and heat, and through this one can judge one's own inherent soul, sun in yourself, where it has come from, which one it is, one can wear the invincible borrowed armour and always remain safe from moral harm in a dark world.

VICTORIES, WAR AND PEACE.

Africa, Kenya, Libya, Nigeria, South Africa
Let me start and confess that me.
And Midas touch are two
Yet must never be twain.
Although we are like two individual loves
We are but one.
Though the touch of Midas always by my
Side

Kenya
How can aurora Borealis
Be subject to an invention
In modern times
Light, laser, brilliant
Bright an Odyssey into great flight
This breath upon its verse
The sweetness of thine
On my arguments so excellent.

Nigeria
Joy happiness, love, truth, beauty.
Joy like a stranger
Went away roaming
Stay near, listen
Nothing resounding
Look Joy is True Love

Coming

Sing, Sing, High Notes and low

Gounod,

Bellini,

Per Pieta,

Stay, Stay Joy,

Do not depart,

Tripping, sweeting, meeting,

Journey's end in Joy

Joy in Grand ascension.

South Africa

The imperfect singer

On stage

The beating heart

The racing pulse

The dry dry mouth and lips

The impresario takes stage.

He directs.

We bow.

And nerves calmed which once,

Were replete.

With raging fear

Stage fright replaced.

With calm and we brace our breath

Once more.

Libya North Africa Egypt North Africa

Dreads depart and never return again.
Dread like the heat of a solar
Flare
Upon my soul
Rages with fury
Like a winter blizzard
The Sceptre, the legislators
Sarbanes Oxley
The world again exorcising.
Its demons one and all
Laying historic ghosts to rest
Sealing them so all ill departs.

South Africa

Cerebrum, Cerebellum,
Medulla Oblongata
The brain stem,
Purkinje fibres
White matter
And Grey
Neurons millions upon millions
In a terrible fray
Thought celestial thoughts.
They enter they exit.

Home sweet Home

My home, my sweet and beautiful home
They come they go,
They enter laughing.
They exit happy,
Oh, what Joy.

The African continent the cradle of creation

Super travel above the beauty below
Laugh, laugh, mirth is here.
with the heat of the almighty sun
Solus Invictus
The furious winter rages of the blue beauty
Below
Sandstorms rising the Sahara Desert
Towards
The Atlantic Canary Islands in grand procession
Arriving between Europe and Africa
The world its task done, slumbers.
He enters so quietly.
The igloos in Alaska
The supersonic movements, consuming all the
Debris of the atmosphere
From backburners aglow
They move so silently so swiftly.
Gone Mach speed missed by all.
Hunted high and low.
Wild beasts

Horses, stallions, elephants, Giraffe, Leopards
Lions Tigers Iguana fair
Lurking in hidden bushes to spring a surprise.
To scorn at danger everywhere
Stealth in action, the Kenyan leopard
The spotted noble Kenyan leopard.

Afghanistan

Once part of India,
The era of the Mughal British Indus
The descriptions of great weight
Beauty strength substance
Blazing heart
Height
Masterful and flet as Mountains of Time

Monologue

Beauty Kindness truth
Variations of a theme
Expressing differences
In argument or verse
What inventions change has brought?
Who is yet oblivious?

Steadfast

The flames surge
As easy as might
The departures unkind

The battle soul weary
The fields of Afghanistan

Date

The end of beauty-
The end of truth
Who says.
Do not my judgements.
Questions from stars
Where all around are predictions of doom.

Tread softly now.

The Lion of all fear
An alliance deadly made,
From fear and dreads
The wires crossed.
Like the glorious sun
He came, please refrain to compare.

The Marble Palace

The ornaments of gold,
The monuments of time
Fountains everywhere
The seas on shore
The hardened stones
The wars they come.

Peshawar, Pakistan, Kashmir
Afghanistan
Overturning all rule of peaceful law.

Afghanistan Victory-
Like a Sea in tempest, I hang my sword.
The birds are silent.
Even when the flute
Sings the snow billows,
Like a sea in tempest, to rest.
Fills my soul.

Grace
Singing she excels
But yet mortal
Dull to cries of terror.
And some British soldiers secretly
In the evening
Their garlands
They bring before this regent so fair.

Strength
Strength in love, no weakness becoming.
Loving less, fighting more, the tongues and songs
Betray
That love was only war begun.

The fighting spirit

That even in hell,

Heaven can be had.

Never perjured,

The mind a gently wind

In deadly battlefields aglow.

The Mountain tops

They freeze.

With snow and ice

The plants forlorn

The flowers lost.

The spring

Like a sea in tempest

To rest, and then while sweet music,

Fills my soul, the art of all around

Creates a killing of all cares,

Of war and sleep footsteps die.

Singing she excels

The awesome dreaded beauty,

Resist, desist, do not comply.

They fear her, sure.

But why?

Fair and sweet,

More noble, they continue in this vein.

It renders seers blind,

They adore her but yet mortal.

Dull to cries of terror, in the evening.
She is a terror to her enemies.

Mighty Love
Strength in love, no weakness becoming.
Spring in every word and phrase
In want, restores,
And greets in woe,
The songs of summer,
Like pipes of war, the days are ripe,
The summer aglow,
The morning begins,
The night in hush,
The boughs laden break, the
Music they cannot bear.
Gone all delight,
Betray not so much more now.
As Love in war.

The Proofs
Purpose, mad in pursuit
Conquests
Reason abandoned.
Limited then restored,
The quests no proof in woe
A Toast proposed,
Behind all dreams
Are you, the world knows Heaven can be had?

In a gentle mind,
As a glow

Rivalry

The Queens, the constant joy,
To win one over, the domestic tempests rage,
Not real friends only feigned,
One day in heaven then back to earth
Home again, as powers exercised did not fail me.
Which one shall I discharge
Vanity all is vanity,
Witty snores,
Intelligence held in contempt.
The comforter, the diplomat,
The other way around,
Who knows,
But I always win.

Straight from Heaven

The golden meadows, the Himalayan mountains
Of God and Glory,
Like sovereign eyes, see.
The golden meadows and we together
Gliding past shining streams
The glories descend like alchemy straight from the
Heavens,
The brilliance of the mighty sun
A carbon copy of me,

Astounding beauty,
Shining like the Morning sun,
Triumphant, proud, splendour
The future I must sustain.
Even on such a beautiful afternoon.

A King's promise never came with a maybe.
I promise I will return again and again.
And he did the space man.
From space, dearest friend
Faithful heart,
Tell her I love her,
She knows,
She always knew,
Ranks in arrange.
Let us beat this foe, the scavenger of time,
Done
Let us make this a beautiful day.

The Immortal war
The world at war
The conquests in sight
Sight and courage.
A dream impossible
Dream
Redeemed the quest.
Not forgotten
Thoughts and heart

The outward glories
The inward glories,
No third time
And no fourth, or fifth
Let us win again and again.

I Return with Care

The victory of one,
Truths proved is a prize.
The pleasures now begin.
I returned with care.
Once again, I swiftly in best form
From mountains and deserts unknown claimed
My own and all that I hold dear.

Time after Time No third Time

The Power is legendary.
This is noble as noble can be.
Otherworldly cosmic a god only for me
Emotions, passions, a royal beginning
In proud array then my six and six
And Kitten cat.
My faithful steed
The birds in spring
They lark they sing.
The eagles soar on mighty wings
A falcon here, a falcon there,
Then a mighty archangel from

Heaven's gates, such beauty
The mountains silently say.
Return home this precious beauty.
Their sweetest and the best

Trumpets

The heart and head,
Dreams aglow roses begin to bloom.
Red, yellow pink and gold
The seasons of snow, return
I want to see you all there,
A head count and all is well.

Pines and Monkey Puzzles

A poet too, of great distinction, this
Calming breeze upon my brow
Now let us sing.

Star crossed voyager bold heart of ours
Here I am.
Speak and let us sing worthless songs.
Our power to unleash,
The angels sing our history.
Past, present and futures.

Unmasked

Perfection rightly graced,
No strength is gone, surgical skills,

The real truth is unmasked,
This then is new life.

Pashtuns

The Pashtuns, advantage upon advantage
The terra firms beside my waters it grows,
Of honours, pride and dignity.
The glories of the lands,
Efficient at revolting,
Brass turns to stone,
Mortality to immortality
The powers of clay, nod here
At this coming.

Paintings of glory

Roses and glory, imitations of the real, the beauty
We strive to indirectly seek, the pills laced with sugar,
Down the roses now mere shadows
The victor restores wealth,
Again, and again and again.

The flag unfurls.
Paradise a place to stay,
We give dues where duty lies,
The eyes see father down winding roads,
Resplendent in the morning glorious sun.

This Sentinel

A clap of thunder,
The stratagems
Napoleon then Claude August,
The Sentinel shows up again and again,
From afar, no epitaph is needed.
No need for revenge,
All is well as it should be.
Have peace of mind.

Glorious quest

Not alone, gods here with gods, titans on green fields
Watchers of time,
Uniforms of gold and silk, like hawks
Obey every question,
Guardians of time
Protections of the highest powers.

Contain the Joy
Immortal thoughts and deeds,
Their heads supreme,
Nature's riches, come and go.
They are our lords of destiny.
Diamond of Solus

A rare stone, glittering celestial light.

Colours hue and height,
This golden one,

It helped me win, the roses.
Grand no thorns on this one.

My Horse is Chestnut Brown
Quickly let us gallop and canter away,
Ten thousand brilliant fields ahead
Time is not fickle,
A call of heaven but returned.
My horse is the wind of the day.

Waxing and waning
The mighty sun is waxing and waning.
The sun is life and is rich.
Its potential is the time of victory,
It is youngest of all suns.

The time of victory
The mighty sun expands.
At the time of victory
To know if I am well,
Trusting it will always do the right thing.
For now, it changes with the times, and
Keeps growing and expanding.

Afghanistan hidden as royal crimson.
The flattery of the gods,
The search can bear,

The immortals be,
A god descends, can this be love.

The Beauty in our midst
The crossing near the Himalayan rivers,
Rest on your laurels,
Tactics,
Strategies,
Acquisitions grow,
We never concede to defeat.
For we are victory.

Canopy was lost.
Obsequious in manner, laying bases to dust.
Form and stealth, like mercy,
So, the motions sound concordance,
The proclamations of Dalhousie.

A Teacher comes.
Reflections with a teacher begin.
The days remain as a solo bird.
In a poplar tree
The time is kind.
Kindness abounds in every form.
The melting snows of Afghanistan,
The repeated irruptions of spiritual
Reality into this world.

Our many previous lives on earth
Preacher of patience,
Preacher of progress
Of enlightenment and immorality-
Six perfections as time,
Giving generosity
Morality
Vigour
Meditation and contemplation
Wisdom
The apparitions of angelic beings,
The defeat of the ultimate enemy
A serene life,
Our true loves all return.
At once and again.

Tree
Wake up from your slumber.
Flight safety laws is the best way.
Finally, Eureka do this.
The expenses
The treasures
Strength is your next door,
Breaking all useless illusions
Remember who you are.
What you have done
Now for that beck and call.

Bliss gold at the end of the rainbow

A reflection,
The noble Aryan race am I born.
Of the mountains the Himalayas
Body mind and all!

JAPAN CHINA, KOREA

Brightest dawn
The brightest dawn
Japan then on the eve of her birth
China could not make up its mind.
Korea some took it as greatest flattery.
Let us unit this Theravadin Buddhist nations.
Glorious man and nation.

Japan Blossoms

Still better now than ever before,
To build on a strong foundation
Stronger and greater
Beyond our wildest dreams
The ideas, the ideals
The fast tempo
Of Japanese brilliant minds.

China rising

Summer awakes and singing.
And stops her stance.
To help me grow into

Something bigger still
These pleasant beckoning's

North Korea and South Korea uniting
Ambitions, ambitions reign supreme.
Ambitions over adversities
Mass demonstrations held.
These fair parades of valour
Transfixed in space and time,
Or is this a pretence,
To us all deceives
No this is the truth.
We must move on.

The Grand Ship of Japan
Freedom, freedom,
Screams inside.
And silently aloud to them
It is not power that corrupts but
Fear of losing power that corrupts.
The outcries consolidated.
Yet beware of reversals. Voyaging on.

Recommendations
The quarters of monks
The doors of simple wood
No dust
No dingy atoms

No clamour and din
The doors they swing open.
Boundaries breaking
Shattering twirling
Whirling whistling
Blowing in the air.

Democracy
In the still ness wisdom appears
By a magnificent tree
I gaze upon it,
With wonder
Culture talks, Japanese,
Chinese, Korean,
Best is democracy, other.
Cultures portrayed.
The cry of the Koreans.

The History
History arrives and the last man comes.
And with it the rise of outcasts
The tears of beggars,
Are heard and troubles,
Lift up and fate is resolved.
Rich now and pregnant with hope.

Untrodden way

China the untrodden way treads,
Her worth is an overwhelming victory.
Her praises silent now,
Only misgivings remain.
Lesser few to love
Hidden away now far away.
This stellar star was but one.

The law safeguards all
Korea under arrest
The law safeguards all
Against all dangers
Like a childish foolish thief
Unrightable wrongs
Critical address,
They return to alleys, woods the simple still.

Iraq the Prelude to Iran

Iraq War in verse
The most formidable time,
The legal intellect of a generation
Uncompromising views her own
Both brilliant and immensely ambitious
Fiercely Loyal
Interests in law and politics,
Both gregarious
Liked the same people.

Enjoyed the same holidays.
Talked the same subjects.
The bedrock of his life,
The very touchstone of his
Independent views
Life spent with one.
Top marks
St Andrews University
The comforts of geology
The courtship then
Over Edinburgh Scottish Hills
And dales
Wandering far and wide
Air Force wife,
Political ambitions
Food for thought
Everywhere the confidence
That Her Aviation husband gave her
She too a fast jet airline pilot swift
Then most
To embolden a seat
At Parliament
A team serving the Queen,
To pay their dues together
At Queens bridge branch together
Elected the general management.
Committee as one
Seeking seats

The trips abroad, the parks
Green and lush
The pale thorough fares
The impact this of one she pilots.
A muse, a wife, a mountaineer
Crystallising his views
Shaping political ambitions
Engendering it
His enemies his own
Allies at home and abroad
Cementing relationships with all
Blair Clinton Bush
The early mornings
Up at dawn before full day break
With Orbs not still wide opened
Still upon the green
The Parliamentarians tall and short
Fat and stout
Lean and mean.
In their smart coats
Ashcroft, Brown,
Still the pivotal role in putting.
Iron in her Husband's soul
The red wine, with Hunter
The assistant
With freckles this she pilots
The Keen air force wife
Never bustling into his meetings

Or intruding into his policies
Supporting
Always Iraq war
The Queen sent her pearly
Greetings of Joy-
The dew drops on scarlet red roses.
Outside
Shone more startling than shocking rubies.
With Dan born when
Rewording a plain
Story from a parliamentary
Score.
Proud energetic
Yet unimaginable constraints
And pressures
Once more then,
Over Scottish hills and London's stores
Knightsbridge
Jenners,
The Chambers
The Inns
And arguments of right and wrong
Just wars,
Always as one
A sure team.

House of commons

Blair Clinton Bush

The House of Commons

June 1983

1983-1989

The Liberals SDP alliance

Margaret Thatcher

Dominant even not

At the height of her power

Labour Michael Foot

1980-1983

Split between supporters.

Tony Ben and the campaign group

On the left

Roy Hattersley and John Smith

The Solidarity group

And Centre left.

Neil Kinnock and the Tribune group

Sedgefield

1983

John Burton

Applying fears to hopes

The people wretched

With closure of mines

Thought an industrial

Revival is required.

Rocky spheres were shaken.

With distractions of Blair

Fairer and faster
Stronger and greater
Burton wise and shrewd
In Labour's way
Making sure Blair
Did not lose with
Middle England
The cracks in invincible stature
Choreographer
Wilson, Trippet, Brooks

Clause IV debate
Captain Stanhope's journey's end Closest
Relationship is with Lieutenant Osborne
Watching over like
Neil Kinnock and Blair
Not the most promising figure
Wilson, Attlee, Gaitskell
Callaghan
Might have been yet.
Looking into the crystal ball
To see which political face is best.
Suited for thee.
A far less impact
The freshness the laughter
Jest at best
Beguiling the world together
Even handed the merits of Brown and Blair

The ensuing leadership
Question
For where is such fierce competitiveness?
Of first among equals born Then not disdaining
One for the other
The tillage of politics this
Forward the clause IV debate.
Did he note the challenges?
Of political posterity
Then then the overwhelming

Doctrine Tradition in peace and conflict
Gould
Mercurial, Strategist,
Behind New Labour
In and out of power
Leaving school with just one
And yet 1985-1992
Labour and its old ways
1992-1997
Modernisation
Losing on tax
Calling back the mornings of April
A phenomenon
A trouble shooter at best
A tireless inspiring encourager
In the third phase
A time for rebuttal

From doctrine tradition
Party
To a values market
Driven the hard truth.
Despite political golden times
This image will not die.
Imperfect circle
The stage set
Not fearing to patch disputes
Or fierce debates
Rejoining replete
Never with sharp rage.
Court's strength
Weakens not for one with Blair.
For everyone with him
Has a place
The fear of trust
The forgotten times
The perfect public services
Fixated on winning.
Fusing all to stay in power
Engine's room's
Foreman's
Strength will not decay.
Overcharged burdens.
Political might
His books, not his eloquence
But strategy speaking forth at best.

The pleading new labour
A new recompense
Form the false tongues.
Expressed of past labours
With new labour a vehicle for key values
Principles and beliefs
Rather than a movement
About class or sectional interest
The court strategist
Certain is new Labour.
The big picture now in focus.

Politics then foreign policy
The man behind the scenes
The screens, the man reshuffles and
Government, appointments
A particular area of focus
More interested in politics than policy
Atlantic Ocean the sea people of Atlantis
Pro-European not
Britain's role should be between the two.
Partisan
Adviser
Blair's master
An eminence grise a voice an echo.
Such politics, legacy, political bequests
Giving much but lending less
His role with the Ecclestone affair

The Times, the disclosures, the pressure
From the top,
Of the civil service and politics
Downing street
Leasing fundraisers
Being frank no abuse
Great on loyalty
Moving political traffic
Alone Powell, no deception
Yet political natures change.
Acceptable one day
Audit's the next day
Left unused the executer comes.
Never real friends
Keeping master's on rails.
Clinton Washington
Clintons of Arkansas
Influence of Clinton
Presidency
Landmark healthcare
Reform bills
Gravitas
High standing ovation
No fears for the heat to come.
The furious storms raging in the
Not so distant futures
The worldly task
Then were that Clinton made?

Much difference to Labour

Yet more impact.

Brown Blair

Home and away

Preparing for power

Between 1994 and 1997

And beyond

Clinton and Blair

Fidele

Resentment in EU grows.

First half of 1998

When Britain held

The EU Presidency

The palpable disappointments

Over key areas of US foreign policy

Kosovo stands out.

Reluctance to do more for the

Good Friday agreement

No great Anglo Americans

Peace initiatives.

In the Middle east or elsewhere

Laws and Diplomacy

Diplomacy and laws

No new globalisation

Or environment concerns

No common stand on

Europe and trade

The new paradigm

Foreign policy
In New York
Exclaimed as utterly brilliant.
The most vacuous
Piece of exposition
Ever heard.
Brown, Hewitt, Milburn
Ed Miliband the best
Absolutely powerful strategies
Golden boys of an era gone
But even in all of this time,
Must now come to rest.

Prescott and the reshuffle
Tensions remained, the frowns of the great
Erupting into the open
Public rebukes of scars on my back
The speech
Care all the more for social revival.
But the swaying of decisions
No collective but bilateral
Byer's departure-
Leading to a reshuffle
The sceptre of Blair
Overseeing regional and local governments
The pivotal broken between
Blair and Brown
Bush and Clinton,

Biden and Trump
Obama and Biden
The learning following this.
The row in April 2004
Over the referendum
EU constitution
Fearing no more instinctively
The steps inside and outside of parliament
For the labour party and the conservatives
The lightning flash of
The Fire brigadier's union
In 2002 and 2003
Admiring Blair's strength
Success all dreaded
Personification of the old and new
Like thunderstones then
Blair and Prescott

Bush and Clinton
Biden and Obama
Trump and Harris
Lashing and punching
Protestors on their jaws
Fearing not censures
Nor slanders
But finishing and consigning
Conservatives, labour,
Democrats and republicans

Hold over.
Then too strong to be.
Dislodged by a stray punch.
Here and a stray punch there
No senators could harm.
Congressmen, nor charm
All laid bear
Anxieties of how
Prescott would interpret.
His deputy Prime Minister
No damage inflicting
On Bush, Clinton, Obama, Harris, Trump, Biden
Prescott would interpret.
His deputy his role
Bringing EU partners
Together on climate change
Or was it really one, with bad things?
Here come not Hiroshima or Nagasaki
But Kyoto
Blair Bush and Prescott.

The Papers of Iraq war and Hunter the Gillian affair.
But lo, the most important
Political event,
Proportionality
Greater influence, than others
Trampling all flood tides
And frontiers, the armies

Forth they come
Never too loud
Their strength
The self-belief
Shaping and affirming
Imperiously continuing to serve and sway

Nontribal instilling hate
Holmes, Heywood, Hunter, Manning Powell
Campbell, Bush, Blair, Clinton, Obama, Trump, Biden, Harris
Not one breaking asunder
The bearing polity
Hands adept
At healing rifts
The hollow ring
Scandals, miry,
Preventing making growing.
Aspirant PM, FM, Kings,
Iron departures
A hole
Every mishap since
The black rod
Episode like Heaven's thunder
Crushing controlling
The falls
Quarrels the media.
The braided gates
Compassing the fallen crests

The epitome of it
From a furnace
Vapours sliding
Scornfully
With false hot image
And disdaining
The ramshackle shuffles
Lambasting taking on,
Scandals the Gillian affair.
The papers of the Mill
Describing the full events

Poisonous man the British public life
The gentle majesty
The modern pride
Anonymous and upright
Captivating eyes, the fairer breed of them all
Summoning her leaves,
Stand by
True worth appreciated.
Here comes the Margaret Thatcher

Cenotaph Margaret Thatcher
Remembrance days come and go.
Services at the Cenotaph
But who will build the present and ongoing?
Looking over the right
This influence so strong

No one can outshine her.
One icon of time,
Education, health, transport,
Comparison from stars and judgements
Kosovo crisis and dilemmas
Of the Falkland's war but not this one,
Only two decades as continuous and four years
On and ongoing, the status
Of her significance in her life
And yet the foundations
Of enduring achievements
Her and his
Performance in foreign policy
Like no one
Such the season's qualities,
Macmillan and Heath
Never registered.
Mesmerising
Use of language
Emphatic leadership
Style intolerant of dissent.
Her authority on the world stage
The futures to come.
Pointing not yet
To coming thunders, rain and wind
These mutual admirations
Society of two
The learning curve

Beginning as early as 1975-1994

Regretting 1987

An unchecked and unbalanced mind

Great achievement of legal frameworks

The Times, Telegraph, and Mail on Sunday,

The admiration of her remained boundless.

But from then on eyes and knowledge arrived

From the vaunting of her as the standard

How you should be judged

Favourable remarks from her on Constance this star

Of fine core strands

Social moralism

Direct democracy, commitment to free markets

Community and Europe

Her determination to win at all costs.

Methods of achieving it

Showing how to ride

Cabinet and parliament

To be bold

To be the purest symbol of symmetry.

Young's biography One of us

Falling for her influence

Her approach to politics

To be in her league

Along with Gladstone, or Lloyd or Gandhi

Attlee, Nehru, Indira, Aung San Suu Kyi, Amrita

And Amritsar, eclipsing them all of them, Jacqueline and K2

She too found her truest heir.
The truest of them all,
A convert to her ideologies.

Campbell the Hutton enquiry darkness descending
The man the image
The approach
Galvanizing communications
But messages across the Hutton enquiry
This impacts policy.
Exaggerated yet the repose of minds.
Foreign travels,
Journeys far and wide
Working political agendas
Diplomacy and laws minds
Thoughts too far and wide
Who believed us strongly?
K2, Sagarmatha, Nanga Prabhat, Kailash Parbat
The soul mountains of God who spoke.
For days and days to Kings of the Cashmere valley
I Am your God to the Greeks, Kashmiris, Nepalese, Tibetans,
Romans, French and English and Scots, the Americans,
The Africans, and so on
Fundamental integrity
Ability to communicate.
With moguls with media
Directing a zealous path
On a political diplomacy and laws map

Drooping eyelids,
Darkness it is descending.
For the blind electoral to see
Campbell, what are you doing?
She a brilliant obsessive
Attack his best form of defence.
The soul merging as two souls on an
Imaginary road, to somewhere
Singapore Mali,
Presenting shadows in forms of sight
The labour jewels
Weary in ghastly nights.
Glares focusing
Rending black
White beauties
New faces for old
Kinnock Kinnock what are you doing?
That part of the shield
Has lost its lustre,
It will ruin you, ensuring
Damaged by near and dear yet on the field.
And straight ahead.

Promise and Jenkins the third way is born!
Jenkins, Jenkins, Jenkins
A time of great opportunity
1995-1998
Political disgrace

And future before a nation's eyes
Cast the mind together!
Europe and the world
Rich in hope
Changing impact, venting frustrations
Slow pace of reform
Jenkins, Rodgers, Williams
Owen,
Bush, Clinton, Biden, Trump Obama, Harris
Endorsements
A symbolic victory
Clause IV Debate 1996-Jenkins
With direct line to the imagination
The tactician running.
Day to day realities
Of parliamentary life
The euphoria of victories,
Features
Friends and politicians
Possessed by diplomacy and laws.
Designing crafts and scopes
Enjoying that those contended with
used and despising.
Coalition all the worth
Grand visions, but broad and vague
Larking at dawn and early breaks
Increasingly frustrated with performance
These interest the single currency.

Reform impact defeat to humming victories.
Downing Street
For the impact of such an alliance
Much wealth should bring, and it did.
She did not like scorn or change of state.
Jenkins died on 5th January 2003.

Polished scripts Mandelson and Clinton
On finding a mission
No other influence
No controversies
Polarising opinions
Intuitively brilliant
Sporadic misjudgements
Fear of years 1985/1997
His new post she like picking up her cast.
Writing polished scripts,
Wetting widows' eyes
Pricking consciences
Promoting issues but haphazardly
Ex General secretary
Mortimer explained.
World is wailing.
Like a hopeless
Encapsulating the prevailing atmosphere
With his pronouncements
Never follow advertising.
In its presentation of politics

We are not as if.
Breakfast food of baked beans
This form never left behind.
With everyone knows swore substance
And more
Not form but eyes see and shape our minds.

Lies and notions.
Yet the wilderness of a strong story
Claiming with had lobbied.
London dome
Such unthrift in the world of spin
Did spend shifting sands.
The vitriol grew and no overnight stay.
As chequers this time,
The cold no longer a voice on the outside
Never missing a heartbeat
The impact as a strategic thinker
A love for him, and a love for her
Love is in the air as love of mine
To build his career
But talent's waste in the world
Must end and all kept unused.
The saving user then destroys it.
No love lost towards one another.
Nor in bosom sits and so on and so on
The murders

With no shame commit
such is the weakest link.

Summit Anderson and swift Bush

The establishment after defeats,
Totally discredited.
Today's hold over
Bias camp now secured.
Forty winters of besieged brows
Now in their trenches
They return.
None other than
Sought out new converts.
To ease the journey to the summit
The beauty of the big news tent
The businessmen
The press
Leaders of the arts world
Royal
Academics
Thinkers
Not forgetting the liberal mind
A new name toasted.
Fewer more illustrious
Unimpeachable figure
Then the youth proud and lively
Gazing on flowering fields of
Great worth ahead

Being asked by all what greatness comes
A teacher a mentor
To celebrated headmaster
Of Eton college
New stalwart
Mentor reality
Fifth generation members
Of an Edinburgh family
Firm of kiltmakers
Watson college
University
First in English
The mentor myth
Stood down to become the treasure of these days.
The deep sunken eyes
Yet to come
The courteous manner
Winning friends
Home and abroad
A seminal figure
In life
The protégé
How much more praise,
Fair the best.
This teacher of mine
Summoning to his court
Slightest excuse
Proving his need

To climb the ladder all the way up
The feeling warm never cold
A mutual and befitting alliance.

Law a passion with Irvine
Launching his career
Grooming his intellect
A face simple but the brain the size
Of the planet
Irvine, law his passion the legal nature
Like own backhanded painted
The master and mistress too of his passion
A gentle heart
A great acquaintance
With shifting times
And fashions
A keen eye to look out.
The false tongues rolling.
Number 10
Dismiss the man with shrewdness.
Judgement
Could others fill?
His shoes without collateral damage
Specialist legal work, as
Lord Chancellor
Much ado about nothing
The next stage of reform, of the House of lords
Reform of the criminal justice system

Promotion of the community legal services
Constitutional reform
Of the judiciary
The plaudits of the legal profession
The second term turbulent
A man of all hues
Not controlling
Stealing eyes
And electorate's souls
Amazed all.
Yet on BBC
Declared he gone soft on crime.
His nature turned an addition now defeated.
Adding not much to purpose
Virtually nothing
But pricked with displeasure.
Defending guidelines
From lord Woolf
The Lord Chief justice
Sentencing guidelines
Fury came.
The catalyst that spelt the end
There and then.

God

God, the most important relationship of all
The dualism of man part earth part cosmos
Few so influenced directly by the cosmos.

Our universal self
Gladstone, -Baldwin, MacDonald,
Callaghan, Wilson, as part man part universe,
Atlantis
So, it was.
The Cosmic Self the muse,
Stirring beauty
God our muse
Always, and forever
Every political verse is God,
Heaven's man and ornament
Rehearsing lines
Complementing the public life
1973
Period of moral reflection
In all political parties
Ancona
The four distinct parts of the cosmos
Nature of the cosmos
Centrality of our Self as universe
A source of solace
The vivid self
The third eye of a visionary
Battling between the arguments
Of outer and inner nature
Relishing pluralism
Intriguing examples
Caught between two worlds.

The age-old dilemma
Right
Expedient
The universe shaping.
Our political thinking
The stress of man his two selves
Outer and inner
God and man
The same
With earth and gems,
With newborn flowers and old
All things common
And all things rare
The helpless
The vulnerable
Stress
Individual has no free will.
The responsibility of Marxism
Predeterminism
Occultism as religious
The quagmire of angels and demons
The demons tell all.
The presence of amorality and morality of man
In their midst tormenting liars to speak the truth
Dangers of the wrong course,
Weapons of mass destruction remote
And satellite leading to alienation.
From the Universe

Iraq war papers accusations
Fly of sanctimony
A charge of annoyance
Another of philosophical weakness
Describing himself as God,
A Robinson Crusoe
Arouses interest.
Bus, Clinton, Obama, Trump, Biden,
Caden
Joan of Arc
Told to go away.
The Dauphin the Heaven's gift
The eve of the Iraq war,
The meeting the goodwill
The speeches of the Young
Saw the gratuitous words of a man.
The Middle East Saudi Arabia, Iran, Pakistan, Afghanistan, Libya
On Italy's shores
G8 Summit in Genoa in 2001
Ireland
Kosovo
Widecombe
Osborne, dissenting.
Morality, Wheatcroft
Writing in Atlantis
Principle the moral right
The notion of natural laws
Misunderstood in time and place.

The road map of the world =
The candles of gold
The rest is hearsay.

Bush
Clinton came.
And left.
Bush rich in rhetoric and promise
Others say no never.
The vision of global Britain and USA
Failed by the vision of the international community.
The perfect dual ceremonies
Iraq war, Iraq war, Iraq war,
weapons of mass destruction
axis of evil
removing dictators the world over
the struggles of Israel and Palestine forgotten by all
the road map
UN resolution 1441
Speaking of love not war
Peace at all costs.
World creative potential
Five thousand on 9/11
See the bigger historical and contemporary picture,
Not just headlines,
Can diplomacy- express?
Proved a far less powerful voice.
Security council office

Bush Cheney,
The promise to be delivered.
No mean feat, strong wits
The Iraq war.
Gordon Brown

Bush and Brown
Blair and Bush
Clinton and Brown
Biden and Cameron
Obama and May
May- and Biden
Rishi and Trump
Rishi and Trump and Biden
Humza Yousef and Trump and Biden
The politicians
The Glorious sun
Drive and ambition.
Gilding blue streams
Brown's innate
No ugly tracks
Brown spreading his wings.
Speaking widely-
On Scots independence
Sturgeon and Salmond
This forlorn visage
Windowless offices
The Euro an issue

Simmering under the surface
1997-2001
Modus operandi
2001-2005 matched in every way.
Skills, character, interest, belief,
marriages
second fiddle
suns and achievement.

Falconer
A Lightning conductor
From Glen Almond
Millennium Dome fiasco,
Stabilising an unsteady ship
Understanding Falconer, Lord Hutton
Judicial chair
The comfort came.

Events

Diana
Churchill in 1940 Diana
Early one morning
Lapsey,
Place de l'Alma,
Paris,
Shook brass, London stones.
The shorelines everywhere

The Royal family,
Leaving an empty world stage
All awash- with grief, shock,
With her infinite love and graces
May still shine.
Like a British beacon bright.

The Good Friday Agreement

The dignity of equality and policy,
Irish flowers blooming sweet.
To live and to die
The past years of dread.

The Euro Decision

European heads of governments
Made it known.
The teeming meeting,
With thoughts of some increase
Bearing the burden
Pound over the Euro.

Kosovo

The Serbian massacre
Kosovo
Albanians
March 24 RAF Tornadoes
With significant effect
Changing fortunes

NATO Secretary General
The thoughts of hate, despise.
Never to think on again
All laws of diplomacy-
The Statutes open.

American Affirmative action
The American take
Affirmative Action
The mortal soul recoiling
The phases
Economic collapses,
The century's new plaques
This is the safer way.

The Iraq war
Operation Desert Fox 1998
Of all they have seen of mead
Flowers,
Butterflies
The summers gay
Yellow leaves
And gossamer
The silver sun
The wind,
Singing on the winds
The winds on the heather

The dossier on Iraq
Wins the day.

Benazir Bhutto
To a fallen sparrow in the fray
Listing all she said and did.
The ship was all to them.
The promise, the hope and all the rest,
When she spoke
She turned and left.
Without a single word
Not tarrying any longer
Her work is done,
The winds are stirring her to the north.
Her final manifesto.

IRAN AND RUSSIA

Antonious George – *The Arab awakening: the story of the Arab national movement* – Philadelphia: Lippincott 1939 Battle for Iraq and Syria in maps – Institute for the study of war via BBC Dec 26 2014 http://www.bbc.com/news/world-middleeast 27838034.

Belts, Alexander and Gil Loescher – *Refugees in International Relations*, Oxford: Oxford University Press 2011.

Gordon Jennifer T – *ISIS' Desire to Erase Sykes-Picot Is Rooted in Fiction, Not History.* The National Interest, September 17, 2014 https://nationalinterest.org/feature/isis-desire-erase-sykes-picot-rooted-fiction-not-history-11293

The Gulf/2000 project: *change, community and co-operation in the Persian Gulf.* School of international and public affairs, Columbia University.

Levitt Matthew – *Regional Implications of the War in Syria* – editorial The Washington Institute, June 2014.

Rose, Gideon *"Gaming ISIS,"* Foreign Affairs. March 22, 2015.

Anna Borshchevskaya – *Syria could be on Trump-Putin agenda, but options for a deal are slim* – Editorial Axios, July 15th, 2018.

Dennis Ross – *Getting Syria Right at the Trump-Putin Summit* – Editorial, interviews, and presentations, July 13, 2018.

Jay Solomon – *North Korea in the Middle East; A Dangerous Military Supply Line* – Editorial Foreign Affairs, June 12, 2018.

Nadav Pollak – *The Israeli Perspective on Safe Zones, in Syria* – Editorial policy watch 2584, March 10, 2016.

Olidort Jacob – *Salafism: Ideas, Recent History, Politics* – Editorial interviews, and presentations – March 2016.

Lt Col John R Barnett – *Establishing and Securing Safe Zones in Syria: Historical Lessons* – Editorial policy watch 2590, March 17, 2016.

REFERENCES

JCPOA

Abolhasan Shirazi Habillah (2015) The nuclear talks of Iran and the United States until the adoption of JCPOA and implementation of Resolution 2231, Volume 8 Issue 30.

Adibadeh Majid (2008) language, discourse and foreign policy, first edition/ Tehran; Nashr-e Akhtaran.

Baeidinejad Hamid step by step with JCPOA – from beginning to end, Tehran Mokharb

Comprehensive Joint Action Plan between the Islamic republic of Iran and the countries of P5+1 Ministry of foreign affairs.

Dehghani Firoozabadi, Jalal – 2013 discourse in the foreign policy of the Islamic republic of Iran Diplomatic Hamshaker Political Analytical Monthly No 74.

Entesar Nadin and Afras Yabi Kaveh (2016) Marathon of Nuclear negotiations from Sababad to Palais Tehran

Hajili Hadi A fsharion modernisation of foreign policy of the 11th government strategic policy research Quarterly year 5 2019.

Jorgensen and Phillips 2002 Discourse analysis London

Lacla Ernst S Moff, Chartal (2013) Hegemony and socialist strategy (towards radical democratic Politics) translated by Mohammad Rezair Tehran.

Hosseini Zadeh Mohammad Ali (2005) Theory of discourse and political analysis political science Number 28.

SANCTIONS

Cordesman A H 92016) Iran after the agreement, in C Cohen S M G Dalton (Eds) Global forecast.

2016 pp30-32 Washington DC centre for strategic and international studies (CSIS).

Grumelli BF and Ivan P (2013) The effectiveness of EU sanctions, European Policy centre (EPC).

Katzman K (2016) Iran's foreign policy CRS report (2015) post sanctions prospects for GCC – Iran Trade in H Ibish (ed)

Wilson T (2015) A flawed deal the centre for the new Middle east (2015) London.

Rennack DE 92015) Iran US economic sanctions and the authority to lift restrictions CRS Report.

The White House (2016) The Iran Nuclear deal what you need to know about the JCPOA Washington retrieved from https://Whitehouse.com

IRAN AND AFRICAN DIPLOMACY

Alchagji, Abbas F (1989) A stakeholder approach to corporate governance managing in a dynamic environment in a dynamic environment, New York, Quantum books.

Blair Margaret M (1995) ownership and control: rethinking corporate governance twenty first centuries, Washington DL: Brooking institute.

Carroll, Archie B (1996) Business and society-, ethical and stakeholder management (3rd edition) Cincinnati, Ohio, Southwestern College publishing.

Cadbury A (1992) – report of the committee, on the financial aspects of corporate governance London; Gee publishing.

Coase, Ronald (1973/1996) – the nature of the firm, in Putterman and Korszer (eds) pp 89-104

Blair Margaret M (1996) – Wealth creation and wealth sharing – A Colloquium on corporate governance and investments in Human capital, Washington, DC Brookings institute.

Blair Margaret M (1995) ownership and control – Rethinking corporate governance for the twenty first centuries, Washington DC, Brookings institute.

Brendt, Markus (2000) – Global differences in corporate governance, systems, theory and implications, for reforms – The Harvard John M, Olin discussion paper series, No 303,

Davidson, Thomas and Lee E Preston (1995) the stakeholder theory of the corporation, concepts, evidence, and implication, Academy of management Review 20 (1) 65-91.

Kay, Jon and Aubrey Silberston (1995) – corporate governance, National institute economic review, August pp 84-96.

OECD (1999) Principles of corporate governance, Paris organisation for economic co-operation and development,

Smith Robert (2003) Audit committees: combined code guidance – a report and proposed guidance by an FRC – appointed group chaired by Smith London; the financing reporting council limited.

Soner Cagaplay – Erdogan's failure on the Nile editorial Cairo review of global affairs, Spring, 2019.

Anna Borschevskaya – Russian activities in Africa in strategic multilayer assessment – May 2019.

Ben Fishman – The conflict in Libya – editorial, congressional testimony, House Committee in foreign affairs May 15, 2019.

Anna Borschevskaya – Moscow in the Middle east and North Africa editorial in House committee on foreign affairs.

Sarah Fever – proceeding with caution in western Sahara – editorial policy watch 3112 April 23, 2019.

Ben Fishman – With interests in Libya under threat, US must adopt urgency.

Alberto Fernandez Sudan- the end comes for Bashir editorial policy notes 62 April 2019.

Simon Henderson – sudden succession essay series, editorial monographs April 2019, ongoing.

Alberto Fernandez – After Bashir's fall, what next for Sudan, editorial policy watch 3103, April 11, 2019.

Sabina Henneberg – Algeria's long build up to mass protests – editorial policy watch 3100

Anna Borscheskay- Russian moves in the Gulf and Africa have common goals, editorial policy alert March 28, 2019.

Anna Borschevskaya – Russia's growing influence in North Africa, Atlantic community Feb 26, 2019.

Ben Fishman – Pompeo's Cairo speech, more back to the future than break with the past editorial The Hill Jan 19, 2019.

Mathew Levitt – Sending the right message in Cairo advice for Secretary Pompeo – Policy watch The Hill% 3063 Jan 7, 2019.

Haslam Hassanin – Egyptian – Israeli Citizenship issues are impeding normalisation, editorial – The Hill, policy alert Jan 3, 2019

Jacob Walles – Tunisia's foreign fighters – editorial – The Hill Policy watch 3053, December 17, 2018.

Ben Fishman – After Palermo, achievements and future challenges for Libya, editorial – The Hill policy watch, 3052 December 17, 2018.

Simon Henderson – Saudi Oil in Iran's crosshairs, editorial Policy alert, The Hill May- 14, 2019.

Michael Knights – an economic roadmap to humanitarian relief in Yemen, Policy watch 3107, April 6, 2019.

Elana Delozier – In Damning Report, UN Panel, details war economy in Yemen, editorial policy, watch 3069, the Hill, Jan 25, 2019.

Nerizbee – The rise of the cyber mercenaries editorial foreign policy, September 2018.

Simon Henderson OPEC nations, including Iran, subject to Moscow – Riyadh divisions, editorial the Hill, June 21, 2018.

Oil – terrorism – Militancy link: Mediatory role of moral disengagement in emergency and crisis management – OP Mafimisebi SEB Thorne – Journal of Emergency – 2015 research portal, Ae, Uk.

Terrorism in Nigeria – group's activities and politics – AB Oyeniyi – International journal of Politics, 2010, Library acendo.net.

BOOKS

Terrorism and oil – N Adams, NJ Adams 2003.

Company law, Ben Pettet, Longman law series, 3rd edition,

Global responses to conflict and crisis in Syria and Yemen – A Guidero McHallward – 2019 Springer Oil and Gas in a new Libyan era – Conflict and continuity – Barltrop R ora.ox.ac.uk.

BOOKS BY AUTHOR - RELATED TO DIPLOMACY AND LAWS

Foreign Affairs – Conceptus Maxima. 2019.

Order of the Defence of Arabia 2019

Bureau Sure Leve 2021

ABOUT THE BOOK

This book addresses diplomacy and laws pertaining to Iran as roman law principles and international laws and is based on them. It is presented as four main key chapters, as prudential, imprudentia, dolus malus as key doctrines, and how these as concepts work on roman legal reforms in the modern context, in the first to last chapter, as seen in the treaty formation, constitution and application of the JCPOA between the USA and Iran, these are more impressionist works rather than a purist academic treatise, it is more conceptual as maxima conceptus and minima, expounds on the legal principle of roman doctrines, and the consequences of treaty application of JCPOA for Iran, when it is enabled. The second chapter is based on the Latin expression casus belli, meaning an event that engages Iran with Russia and provokes them both to justify ending a civil war in Syria literally and metaphorically, and how they make this case, as casus belli comes into play and involves both Russia and Iran as two main key players acting out diplomacy and laws in an international arena such as Syria in Arabian peninsula, the poetical expressions explore, the thinking and philosophies on a day to day basis in a modern Damascus, where both nations under their leaders are compelled to follow through and save it from a catastrophic fall, this is more than a legal treatise and explores key seminal events, as casus belli doctrine in Syria. Finally, the final part of the book presents Iran, Arabia and African laws and diplomacy which hinge on the exploration of oil and gas through this vast arena, and where principles of laws, norms and philosophy come to the fore and from which no derogation is permitted as corporate, company, national laws, legislation and humanitarian laws, how Iran is forced to engage with these as is Africa before her, then Arabia and now the Iranian nation one of the riches with gas reserves in the world. The book contains a philosophical slant as expressed on the wars in Afghanistan, Libya, Iraq and spilling as far, as China, Taiwan, Korea and Japan.

The diplomacy and laws of Iran with each nation USA and Russia are evidenced as mutually explosive one, hostile and another aligned and friendly to her cause and development through gas exploration, marketing as a way forward to develop Iran post the enlightenment of the Persian empire, as one in a place of darkness and destitution.

ABOUT THE AUTHOR

Dr Amrit Rattan K Baidwan Macfarland – the Author primarily trained as Scientist at her universities in Physics its impact on Molecular genetics and conducted research in cell membrane genetics, signalling and transduction systems, collaborating with Jefferson Medical School in Philadelphia and NIH Bethesda Washington State. After obtaining her doctorate, she taught and researched extensively in molecular genetics and biomedical sciences. She entered the legal profession and trained as a lawyer with a highly reputable international firm, dealing with international solemn supreme court cases in criminal litigation and terrorism legislation, she also worked as a chamber practice lawyer and applied her masters (First with distinction in her dissertation both) in international laws and intellectual property laws in many cases. Her Masters specialism in foreign affairs, peace and conflict, international relations (Thesis Napoleonic wars, to world war I and world war II, cold wars to wars on terrorism in Africa, Arabia, Asia Major, Asia Minor and Afghanistan); serves as a foundation for many of her books in International Diplomacy and Laws. She undertook the study of comparative laws in UK and the USA, (Juris Doctorate subjects) constitutional laws, criminal laws, corporate laws, international laws, civil and criminal justice legal reforms with Summa cum laude visiting professors from Washington State, Harvard, Princeton, Cornell Yale universities from the main corpus Juris of main universities of Washington State, Baltimore, and Maryland. Her thesis in press and papers examined were based on the death penalty reforms, presented orally and examined by Legal of Counsel, Associate Professor and accredited by the American Bar Association body. To date she has written three book on International diplomacy and laws, on the Russian Ukraine conflict in Europe, a second on the One Taiwan China doctrine and this on USA and Russian diplomacy and laws and Iran.

www.ingramcontent.com/pod-product-compliance
Lightning Source LLC
LaVergne TN
LVHW012245070526
838201LV00090B/125